Prophetic Preaching

A Pastoral Approach

Leonora Tubbs Tisdale

WESTMINSTER
JOHN KNOX PRESS
LOUISVILLE · KENTUCKY

© 2010 Leonora Tubbs Tisdale

First edition
Published by Westminster John Knox Press
Louisville, Kentucky

10 11 12 13 14 15 16 17 18 19—10 9 8 7 6 5 4 3 2 1

Scripture quotations from the New Revised Standard Version of the Bible are copyright © 1989 by the Division of Christian Education of the National Council of the Churches of Christ in the U.S.A. and are used by permission.

See "Permissions," pp. 107–8, for additional permissions information.

Book design by Drew Stevens
Cover design by Pamela Poll Design

Library of Congress Cataloging-in-Publication Data

Tisdale, Leonora Tubbs.
    Prophetic preaching : a pastoral approach / Leonora Tubbs Tisdale. — 1st ed.
        p. cm.
    Includes bibliographical references and index.
    ISBN 978-0-664-23332-7 (alk. paper)
    1. Preaching. 2. Prophecy—Christianity. I. Title.
    BV4211.3.T57 2010
    251—dc22

                                                                    2010003672

♾ The paper used in this publication meets the minimum requirements of the American National Standard for Information Sciences—Permanence of Paper for Printed Library Materials, ANSI Z39.48-1992.

Westminster John Knox Press advocates the responsible use of our natural resources. The text paper of this book is made from 30% post-consumer waste.

For my parents,
Leonora Cousar Tubbs and James Balfour Tubbs,
who first taught me to love God and the Scriptures,
and whose lives of faith and faithfulness
have been an inspiration to many

1200

127560

Contents

Acknowledgments   vii
Introduction   ix

1. Where Have All the Prophets Gone?   1

2. Rekindling the Fire Within: A Spirituality
   for Prophetic Witness   21

3. Speaking Truth in Love: Strategies
   for Prophetic Proclamation   41

4. Giving Shape to the Witness: Forms
   for Prophetic Preaching   63

5. Word *and* Deed: The Integrity of Prophetic Witness   89

   Permissions   107
   Notes   109
   Bibliography   121
   Index   127

Acknowledgments

Books are communal endeavors, and this one no less than others. Its seeds were first sown in my childhood, especially by my mom and dad to whom this book is dedicated. They were the ones who first taught me to love the Christian Scriptures, and it was through their preaching, teaching, and nurturing care that I first came to know and love the God of compassion and justice to whom the biblical stories give testimony. My parents have not only been faithful, consistent witnesses to me of God's abundant grace; they have also modeled for me through the years how to speak truth in love.

In my youth and young adult years, I was inspired by a number of prophets—both local and global—who courageously spoke truth to church and nation during a time of struggle for civil rights, an ongoing and ill-devised war in Southeast Asia, and governmental deception and its cover-up. While some of their names were writ large—names like Martin Luther King Jr., Rosa Parks, and William Sloane Coffin—others were known only to local communities of faith, where they sometimes paid a high price for their truth speaking in the name of God. (See the introduction for the names of some of my local prophetic heroes.) I still remember pastors who were subjected to vicious hate mail, accused of being anti-American, or forced to leave their pulpits because they dared to speak out on behalf of racial justice, honest government, and peace in our world. Their witness has long made me want to be more faithfully prophetic, too.

In more recent years I have been inspired by the students and faculty at Yale Divinity School—many of whom are making a difference in this world through their own commitments to peacemaking and justice seeking. I count it a privilege to live and work in their midst.

This book has been many years in the birthing, and along the way I have given lectures related to it at Pittsburgh Theological Seminary (Schaff Lectures), at the ACTS Doctor of Ministry in Preaching program in Chicago (Wardlaw Lectures), and at continuing education events for pastors. The stories pastors have told me and the questions

I have been asked on those occasions have helped make this a better book.

I am grateful to Yale Divinity School and to its dean, Harold Attridge, for allowing me a sabbatical in the spring of 2009 so that I could finally bring this book together. I also extend gratitude to my Yale colleague in preaching, Thomas Troeger, for his constant encouragement and support, and to Neichelle Guidry and Andrea Burr, who served as my able research assistants. A special thanks goes to the "Sisters of Spirit," a group of women pastors who bonded in a course I taught on women and preaching over twelve years ago, and who graciously agreed to read a penultimate draft of this book in order to give me wise and insightful feedback on it.

Finally, I thank my beloved husband of thirty-five years, Alfred, and our children for their constant love, support, and encouragement. I became a grandmother for the first time while writing this book, and I pray that little Madeline will grow up in a world where the prophets are not afraid to raise their voices and where a vision of God's justice, peace, and equality is proclaimed from the rooftops.

Nora Tubbs Tisdale
Pentecost season, 2009

Introduction

Recently I returned to the city in North Carolina, where I grew up, to preach and give a lecture at a local church on prophetic preaching. It had been many years since I had spent any significant time in my hometown, so the trip also afforded me an opportunity to stroll down memory lane. I spent an afternoon with an old high school friend, reminiscing about the good times we had shared in our teen years. I drove by the house where my family lived when I was a little girl and marveled at how much smaller it seemed in reality than in my memory. I saw the neighborhood elementary school I attended and remembered how the walk home from school often seemed much longer than it actually was. And I marveled at all the changes that had occurred in that city since I moved away forty years ago.

As my friend and I reminisced, the topic that was foremost in our conversation was race relations in that city and how deeply they affected us during our high school years. We both remembered how, in our junior year of high school, our city had finally fully integrated its high schools by closing down the all-black high school, located only a few blocks from the predominantly white school, and merging the two. Needless to say, such a move did not promote good will on the part of many of our classmates.

Later that same year Martin Luther King Jr. was assassinated. In the wake of his death, the pent-up frustrations resulting from centuries of oppression erupted in racial protests of both a violent and nonviolent nature that tore our city asunder. National Guard troops were called in to keep the peace, and many were the nights when the whole city was under a strictly enforced curfew. My friend and I agreed that when we remembered our high school days, it was always with a thick overlay of racial tension and unrest.

If truth be told, our college years were no less conflicted. In addition to the ongoing struggle for civil rights, the Vietnam War was raging, protesting college students were killed by National Guard troops at Kent State University, and the Watergate cover-up and Richard

Nixon's subsequent impeachment were testing the limits of our nation's democracy. It was a difficult time to be coming of age in our land. As a young adult who was also a Christian, I hungered for the church to be a prophetic witness in the midst of those times. I longed for a church that would speak to me not only about personal faith and piety but also about the key events that were going on in city, nation, and world, and I wanted a church that would help me discern what we as Christians should believe and do in the midst of them.

My favorite Christmas carol during those days was "I Heard the Bells on Christmas Day." I was drawn to it because its penultimate stanza echoed my own growing sense of despair in the face of war, racial prejudice, governmental deception, and violence, and also because its final stanza strongly spoke of the hope at the heart of the Christian gospel:

> And in despair, I bow'd my head:
> "There is no peace on earth," I said,
> "For hate is strong and mocks the song
> Of peace on earth, good will toward all."

> Then pealed the bells more loud and deep
> "God is not dead nor doth God sleep;
> The wrong shall fail, the right prevail
> With peace on earth, good will to all."[1]

It was no accident, then, that my heroes in my young adult years tended to be prophets—both of my own (Presbyterian) denomination and of other denominations—who, by their words or deeds, were willing to address the issues of our day in honest, complex, and hope-filled ways. I think, for instance, of Dr. Bernard Boyd, the small, wiry religion professor at the University of North Carolina who first introduced me to the Old Testament prophets and the challenges they posed for faithful Christian living. I think of Dr. Albert Curry Winn, my pastor during my seminary years in Richmond, Virginia, who gave away much of his annual income so that he would not have to pay taxes that would support the Vietnam War and who also preached regularly and passionately about peace and peacemaking. I think of noted African American pastors—such as Dr. Joe Roberts, then pastor of Ebenezer Baptist Church in Atlanta—who challenged and inspired me with their truth speaking at church conferences. And I think of Rev. Neil McMillan, the humble, soft-spoken pastor of my hometown congregation who dared pray for the North as well as the South Vietnamese during Sunday morning worship services.

I was also deeply moved by the witness of prophets in South Korea during the year (1977 to 1978) that my husband and I served as volunteer missionaries, teaching at the Presbyterian Theological Seminary in Seoul. South Korea at that time was governed by a right-wing president, Park Chung Hee, who preyed on the fears of the people to foster a rampant militarism, and whose government made it illegal for anyone to speak out publicly against it. I still remember sitting in a living room in Seoul and hearing Drs. Timothy and Steven Moon, two brothers who were also biblical scholars and were newly released from prison, tell about the theologies of joy they had each written while serving long months in separate solitary confinement for their outspokenness against the government. I felt that I was in the presence of two modern-day apostle Pauls. I also remember sitting on a pew at the open-air Galilee Church that met on a hillside in Seoul—a church frequented by families of political prisoners. These families would gather together to share news of their relatives in prison and to have their faith bolstered through worship, and as I listened to their testimonies of faith, members of the Korean CIA sat on the back pew, taking notes. That small congregation always closed their worship service by joining hands in a circle in the front of the church and singing hymns and protest songs such as "Oh, Freedom" and "We Shall Overcome." But they never began their singing until they had first invited the CIA agents to join their circle.

Why was I drawn to these Christians and to their prophetic witness? I was drawn to them for at least two reasons. First, they dared to speak honestly about what was going on in that day—and to wrestle with those issues in the context of the Christian faith. With them the Christian faith was not irrelevant; it had a significant and meaningful word to proclaim not only to individuals but also to city, nation, and world.

Second—and most important—these prophets also spoke of the hope God offers to us in the biblical vision: hope of a new day to come when people would beat their swords into plowshares and their spears into farming implements; hope of an era when we would not judge human beings by the color of their skin but by the quality of their lives; hope of a coming time when wolf and lamb would lie down together and children would safely play without fear of harm.

In his classic book *The Prophetic Imagination,* Old Testament scholar Walter Brueggemann speaks of the hopeful nature of prophetic witness in the biblical story. Prophetic witness, he maintains, is inherently countercultural, and the prophets of old evoked such a countercultural consciousness by the use of two different languages. First, they *criticized* the old order, pronouncing God's judgment upon it. And second, they *energized* their hearers with a vision of the new reign of God that was to come.[2]

It was, of course, the criticizing that was the tough part because people did not then, and still do not today, want to be shaken out of their numbness, complacency, and self-deception in order to see themselves, their nation, and their world the way God sees them. But Brueggemann also reminds us that "the riddle and insight of biblical faith is the awareness that only anguish leads to life, only grieving leads to joy, and only embraced endings permit new beginnings."[3] It is only as we recognize the necessity of the old order coming to an end, only as we lament and grieve its certain passing, that we can be opened to God's energizing vision of a new order to come.

I am drawn to prophetic witness, in the first instance, because I believe that the prophets of God—both in ancient times and today—have been harbingers of hope, naming reality as it is and placing before us a vision of the new future God will bring to pass.

But I am also drawn to this topic because I found during my years as a parish pastor—first as copastor with my husband in a parish of four small churches in Central Virginia, and then more recently while serving on the staff of Fifth Avenue Presbyterian Church in New York City—that prophetic preaching was the hardest kind of preaching I did. And I have been on a lifelong quest to learn how to do it better.

At the heart of the difficulty, I believe, is the fact that parish pastors, unlike most Old Testament prophets, are called to be both priests and prophets to their people. And living within that tension is often difficult. How do you speak hard words of judgment from God, often controversial words, to a people you dearly love in a way that does not shut down your relationship with them? And how do you walk that delicate tightrope in ministry between pastorally building up people who have been beaten down in life while also prophetically calling them to live responsibly in relation to others who have been beaten down by this world, its peoples, and its systems?

If truth be told, I am writing this book not because I've got it all together but because I, like many others in the church, am still struggling with what it means to be a faithful prophetic witness in the present day. So I want to share some things I'm learning along the way, while also acknowledging that I still have a lot to learn.

Finally, I have a strong interest in this topic because of scholarly research I have undertaken in recent years. One of the great gifts of my academic life was the opportunity to work for three years with an interdisciplinary team of scholars who were commissioned to write the history of The Riverside Church in New York City in celebration of that church's seventy-fifth anniversary.[4] The team, headed by ethicist Peter Paris, also included a sociologist, two historians, a professor of art and architecture, and me, a homiletician. My assignment—the best portion, I thought—was to write the chapter on the preaching and worship life of Riverside Church. So I spent months in the archives of that great church, researching the lives and reading or listening to the sermons of the first five Riverside preachers: Harry Emerson Fosdick, Robert James McCracken, Ernest T. Campbell, William Sloane Coffin Jr., and James A. Forbes Jr.

I came away from that project deeply inspired by the witness of these five faithful, prophetic preachers—each of whom used his own unique gifts, life experiences, and theological perspectives to bring a prophetic word to church and nation from that great pulpit. I learned a lot about how to preach prophetically simply by reading their sermons and by witnessing the diverse ways that they preached.

But I also came away challenged. One of the striking things about the Riverside sermons is that you can literally read the history of our nation and world through them. And I know of few other pulpits today where that is the case. Reading those sermons caused me to ask, Where have all the prophets gone? Why do churches and pastors so often seem to shy away from prophetic witness?

This book is my attempt to address those questions and to provide guidance and encouragement for pastors who want to recommit themselves to the task of prophetic witness. In the process I will wrestle with how pastors can proclaim God's prophetic Word in more pastoral ways within local communities of faith. My goal here is not to water down the gospel so that it becomes more palatable to local congregations. Rather, my goal is to discern how preachers can "speak truth in love" in ways that enable congregations to genuinely hear and respond to that Word. I will also address the challenges that prophetic preaching presents for the pastor's own life—both in terms of the spiritual resources and practices that are necessary for supporting and undergirding prophetic ministry and in terms of the kinds of deeds and actions that are required of those who would be faithful prophets of God.

I begin in chapter 1 by addressing the question "Where have all the prophets gone?" and identifying a number of reasons why pastors today tend to avoid prophetic witness. My own belief is that the avoidance of prophetic witness is at heart a spiritual problem. I thus outline in chapter 2 the parameters of what a "spirituality for activism" (a phrase I borrow from Rev. James A. Forbes Jr.[5]) might look like for today's preachers. In chapter 3, I tackle the question "How can ministers of the gospel be both pastoral and prophetic at the same time in their preaching?" I will discuss a number of strategies for prophetic preaching that also attend to the pastoral needs and concerns of the congregation. In chapter 4, I turn my attention to forms for prophetic preaching, examining both classic forms and newer ones and suggesting a diversity of ways that a preacher can structure a prophetic sermon. And in chapter 5, I talk about the intersection of word and deed in prophetic witness, including the challenge prophetic preaching poses for both the preacher's own lifestyle and the congregation's corporate witness in the world.

At the outset let me state that my vantage point for thinking about these concerns stems from my own life experience, as both a pastor and a parishioner, in congregations that have tended to be predominantly white, middle to upper class, and located in a diversity of contexts (urban, suburban, small town, and rural).[6] While these congregations have varied greatly in size—ranging from 36 to 3600 members, the reality is that I have preached more to the haves than the have-nots, and often to people who are leaders in their communities. Consequently, the goals of prophetic ministry in my context are not so much to lift up and empower the oppressed as they are to challenge and encourage action on the part of those who have the power to make change happen. Or, to put it in more popular parlance, prophetic witness is more about "afflicting the comfortable" than "comforting the afflicted."

My hope and prayer is that this volume may encourage more pastors to take up the mantle of prophetic ministry so that they, in turn, may empower local congregations to become bolder prophetic witnesses in church and world. For in the end, the task of prophetic witness and ministry does not ultimately belong to the pastor; it belongs to the entire community of faith.

1

Where Have All the Prophets Gone?

God was saying to me, "witness to this," and "reveal the truth about this," and "be a prophet." And I said, "No, thank you. I don't want it!"

[God] said, "This will be a great service to people you love, to tell them the truth."

And I said, "They're not going to thank me for it. I know that for sure. People hurt prophets. They throw sharp things at them. . . . I don't want that. I don't want any pain whatsoever. . . . Minor dentistry is more than enough for me."

So no thank you, I don't want to be a prophet and tell the truth. What can I do that's the opposite of that? And so I got into this line of work: telling lies.[1]

Garrison Keillor, "Prophet," *Fertility* CD

In his book *Where Have All the Prophets Gone?* Marvin McMickle—who is both pastor of Antioch Baptist Church in Cleveland, Ohio, and professor of preaching at Ashland University—takes American pastors to task, claiming that many of us have sold out the God of biblical justice for a lesser god and, in so doing, have blunted or silenced the prophetic voice of the American pulpit.

Several things, McMickle claims, have contributed to the demise of prophetic preaching in churches of his own African American tradition, including

1. an overzealous preoccupation with the place of praise in some churches and services of worship (which has resulted in pastors' downplaying or ignoring the pain and suffering of our world);
2. a false and narrow view of patriotism (that has sometimes equated unqualified praise of country with love of country); and
3. a focus in preaching on personal enrichment themes or a prosperity gospel to the exclusion or detriment of the gospel's broader social justice claims.[2]

Both conservatives and liberals alike have contributed to the demise of prophetic preaching, says McMickle, in that both have tended to be one-issue preachers when it comes to preaching justice—with conservatives focusing primarily on "family values" and abortion, and with liberals primarily focusing on human sexuality and gay rights. In the process, he claims, a host of other important justice issues have gone largely unaddressed and underacknowledged in the American pulpit, such as immigration reform, global warming, the war in Iraq, the scourge of illegal drugs in our cities, both global and local poverty, health-care reform, the AIDS crisis, the ever-growing prison population in our land, and ongoing racism and sexism.

What McMickle sounds in this book is a clarion call for preachers who will rise up and boldly take on the mantle of prophetic preaching and who will respond to the call of Isaiah 6:8 ("'Whom shall I send, and who will go for us?'") by saying, "'Here am I; send me!'" He writes,

> It is still our task to call people back from the worship of Baal and other idols, but we will need to attach twenty-first century identities to those false gods. It is still our task to demand that society care for "the least of these" among us, but we will have to attach twenty-first century names and faces and conditions to those persons. It is still our task to speak truth to power and stand against the forces of injustice as they appear not only within the broader reaches of American society, but also as they manifest themselves within the life of the contemporary church.[3]

Consequently, he says, "we need an understanding of prophetic preaching that matches the times in which we live: a postmodern, nuclear-terrorist, politically polarized, grossly self-indulgent age, in which all the world's citizens reside in a global community."[4] And we need preachers who are willing to take on this mantle and rise to the challenge of prophetic preaching, as difficult as it might be.

McMickle is honest in saying that he doesn't think all preachers will respond positively to this call. Indeed, he says that the recovery of prophetic preaching and prophetic action will likely begin with a *remnant*, a small vocal minority who take this call seriously.[5] But he also looks back over our nation's history and reminds us that in former times of crisis such prophets have arisen, and while their voices have not always been popular at the time, they have made a significant difference in shaping the collective conscience and actions of church and of nation. He is hopeful that in our day as well God will raise up such a remnant.

I, too, am hopeful that God will raise up such a remnant. But if that is to happen, we as preachers will first need to wrestle honestly with why it is we avoid or fear prophetic preaching, and we need to come clean about our own resistances in this regard. Why is it that we are sometimes tempted to substitute another god for the God of justice of the Scriptures? Why do we avoid speaking truth in love regarding some of the burning issues of our day? And why are we often fearful of what becoming prophetic witnesses will mean for our lives?

In this chapter, I will begin addressing those questions. But first it is important to define prophetic preaching and to describe its attributes so that we have some clarity regarding what it is that we are discussing.

WHAT IS PROPHETIC PREACHING?

When I mention to friends and acquaintances that I am writing a book on prophetic preaching, the first question I am usually asked is "What do you mean by that term?" If truth be told, that is a highly reasonable question because "prophetic" is currently used in church circles in ways that can be confusing and even conflicting.

For example, if you search the Internet for "prophetic" sermons, you will find that the reference is often used in regard to sermons that in some way either predict the future or deal with the end times. These sermons, often rooted in literalistic modes of biblical interpretation, tend to be based on apocalyptic texts from the Bible—such as those found in the book of Revelation or the "little apocalypse" in Mark— or on passages from the Old Testament prophets that "foretell" the coming of the Messiah. They bear titles such as "Preparing for the End Times," "Is the Rapture for Real?" or "Who Is the Beast?"

On the other hand, in many mainline church circles the term *prophetic* usually refers either to preaching based on prophetic biblical texts that call people to live into God's vision for justice, peace, and equality in our world (such as those found in the Hebrew prophets or the teachings of Jesus), or to preaching that addresses significant social issues and concerns. It is the kind of preaching that can "get ministers in trouble" with their congregations because it often goes against societal norms, pronouncing not only grace but also God's judgment on human action or inaction.

While recognizing with respect the many Christians who gravitate toward the former understanding of "prophetic preaching," this book's focus will decidedly be on the latter understanding of the term. I am interested in the type of preaching that is cutting edge and future oriented (yet not future predicting), and that addresses public and social concerns. However, having stated that bias, I also acknowledge that even among homileticians who share it, there is no unanimity regarding how to define the term—or even whether to use it. What emerge instead are certain hallmarks that characterize this important mode of proclamation and that help differentiate it from other types of preaching. It is to a consideration of those hallmarks and to the diverse definitions given for "prophetic preaching" that we now turn our attention.

Philip Wogaman's Definition

Philip Wogaman, a Christian ethicist who also served for many years as pastor of Foundry United Methodist Church in Washington, DC (and who was pastor to the Clintons during their White House years), gives a rather broad definition of prophetic preaching in his book *Speaking the Truth in Love*. He writes, "To be prophetic is not necessarily to be adversarial, or even controversial. The word in its Greek form refers to one who speaks on behalf of another. In Hebrew tradition, a prophet is one who speaks for God. . . ." [6] He goes on to ask, "What does it mean to speak for God?"[7]

The prophet has a singular grasp of what God intends. Through the prophets the people have a window into the reality of God and how the reality of God can shape and direct their existence. He cites James Russell Lowell's poem "Columbus," a portion of which, though written in a different context, is suggestive:

> For I believed the poets; it is they
> Who utter wisdom from the central deep,
> And listening to the inner flow of things,
> Speak to the age out of eternity.[8]

"This is exactly the job description of the prophet," says Wogaman. "To speak for another is to grasp, first, the mind of the other . . . genuinely prophetic preaching draws people into the reality of God in such a way that they cannot any longer be content with conventional wisdom and superficial existence."[9]

Dawn Ottoni-Wilhelm's Definition

Dawn Ottoni-Wilhem, professor of preaching at Bethany Christian Seminary in Indiana and a scholar who approaches preaching from an Anabaptist "peace church" tradition, helpfully reminds us that the prophetic tradition in which we stand is not only the tradition of the Old Testament prophets; it is also the tradition of the prophet Jesus.

> In accordance with the prophetic tradition of Israel and the ministry of Jesus Christ as recorded in Scripture, prophetic preaching may be understood as divinely inspired speech enlivened by the Holy Spirit in the gathered community of faith. Prophetic preaching proclaims God's Word from within the Christian tradition against all that threatens God's reconciling intention for humanity and for all that creates and sustains a vital and necessary ministry of compassion to neighbors near and far. Because it is not exclusively either moral exhortation or predictions regarding future events, prophetic preaching envisions past, present and future concerns within the context of the reign of God realized in Jesus Christ and empowered by the Holy Spirit.[10]

Ottoni-Wilhelm differentiates prophetic preaching from both "moral exhortation" and "predicting the future" and reminds us that even as prophetic witnesses must stand *for* all that creates and sustains a ministry of compassion to neighbors near and far, they also must stand *against* all that threatens God's good intention for creation. She also reminds us that prophetic preaching must be undertaken in the Spirit of Christ, reflecting his compassion for the world and its brokenness.

Ottoni-Wilhelm names three essential elements of prophetic preaching that can be discerned from considering Jesus' own prophetic words and deeds. First, *prophetic preaching voices God's passion for others.* It incarnates and gives voice to God's love for the world revealed in Christ Jesus and using the language of lament, voices God's deep sorrow over evil and injustice. Second, *prophetic preaching proclaims the promises of God.* The prophet announces the coming reign of God, which has already broken into our midst in Jesus of Nazareth, and gives assurance that God's promise of a new day of justice and peace and equality will surely come to pass. And third, *prophetic preaching points the way to new possibilities.* Using the language of imagination, it invites us to envision the new day God intends and to discern how God would creatively use us to help bring that day to completion.[11]

Social-Justice Preaching, Public-Issues Preaching, and Liberation Preaching

While Wogaman and Ottoni-Wilhelm begin with the biblical witness in defining prophetic preaching (Wogaman with the witness of the prophets of the Hebrew Scriptures and Ottoni-Wilhelm with the witness of the prophet Jesus), other authors in the field of homiletics, while writing about prophetic preaching, don't actually define it. Instead they use the term interchangeably with phrases such as "social-justice preaching," "liberation preaching," or "public-issues preaching."

For example, when Kelly Miller Smith gave the Lyman Beecher Lectures on preaching at Yale Divinity School in 1983, he focused them around the theme of "social crisis preaching."[12] When Catherine and Justo González authored a book about prophetic preaching from their vantage point as Hispanic Americans, they titled it *Liberation Preaching*.[13] And when Christine Smith gathered an ethnically diverse group of authors to write about preaching out of the context of oppression as their various communities had experienced it, she titled it *Preaching Justice*.[14]

While prophetic preaching is certainly, as Wogaman rightly indicates, any preaching that "speaks for God," authors who use terms like prophetic preaching and social-justice preaching and liberation preaching interchangeably press us to acknowledge that to speak for God also means to speak on the cutting edge of what is just and what is unjust in the local communities in which we find ourselves; to bring God's Word to bear on key events and at crisis moments in the life of church, nation, and world; and to have a bias in our preaching toward the liberation of God and the upending of powers and principalities, thus bringing in a reign marked by peace and equality and justice for all.

Walter Brueggemann's Definition

Lest we become too comfortable equating prophetic preaching with preaching on social or political issues, biblical scholar Walter Brueggemann reminds us that ultimately there is something far bigger at stake. When the biblical worldview and our own cultural worldviews come into collision, Brueggemann insists, an entire change of perception and consciousness is required on the part of those who would attend to God's Word. He offers his own definition of prophetic ministry in his now-classic book *The Prophetic Imagination*: "The task of prophetic ministry is to nurture, nourish, and evoke a consciousness and perception alternative to the consciousness and perception of the dominant culture around us."[15]

Brueggemann continues:

Thus I contend that prophetic ministry has to do not primarily with addressing specific public crises but *with addressing, in season and out of season, the dominant crisis that is enduring and resilient, of having our alternative vocation [as Christians] co-opted and domesticated.* It may be, of course, that this enduring crisis manifests itself in any given time around concrete issues, but it concerns the enduring crisis that runs from concrete issue to concrete issue. That point is particularly important to ad hoc liberals who run from issue to issue without discerning the enduring domestication of vision in all of them.[16]

For Brueggemann, prophetic witness is not primarily about addressing social or political issues, as important as it might be for preachers to do so. Rather, it is fundamentally about calling us as people of God to a radical reorientation of our worldview and consciousness so that we see and perceive the world as God sees it and have our hearts break over the things that break God's heart. Such preaching is inherently countercultural, for God frequently views our social orders and institutions as being corrupt and in need of transformation. But it is also hopeful, because through such proclamation we set before the people of God a new vision of an eschatological reality yet to come—a reality God is even now creating in our midst.

Marvin McMickle's Definition

In his book *Where Have All the Prophets Gone?* Marvin McMickle acknowledges his own resonance with Brueggemann's definition of prophetic preaching:

This approach to prophetic preaching is consistent with what Walter Brueggemann in his book *The Prophetic Imagination* calls "prophetic consciousness." He writes that the work of the prophet is to be able to project before the people "an alternative future to the one the king wants to project as the only thinkable one." For Brueggemann, the Old Testament prophets had to contend with what he calls "royal consciousness." This "royal consciousness" represents the deeply entrenched forces—political, economic, social or religious—of Israel. They are the status quo, and they only offer to people a vision of the future that allows them to remain in power and requires that the masses of people remain marginalized in society. The work of the prophet is to combat that single vision and show that God can and will bring about a future different from that envisioned by the ruling elite.[17]

McMickle goes on to note that prophetic preaching must be undertaken with both hope and humility:

> As Abraham Joshua Heschel wrote in his classic book *The Prophets,* "prophetic preaching must be endowed with 'divine pathos.'" Heschel states, "The prophets communicated God's anger over the sins of the covenant community. However, what God intends is not that his anger should be executed, but that it should be annulled by the people's repentance." In the final analysis, it is hope and deliverance, not death and destruction, that are the ultimate objectives of prophetic preaching.[18]

John McClure's Definition

John McClure, professor of preaching at Vanderbilt Divinity School, offers this definition of prophetic preaching in his book *Preaching Words*: Prophetic preaching is *"an imaginative reappropriation of traditional narratives and symbols for the purpose of critiquing a dangerous and unjust present situation and providing an alternative vision of God's future."*[19]

While McClure draws on Brueggemann's understanding that prophetic witness involves both criticizing the old order and providing a new alternative vision of God's new future, he also reminds us that prophetic preaching brings together sacred biblical texts (and their traditional narratives and symbols) and the present situation (and its injustices) in imaginative ways. It is from the sacred narratives and traditions of the Christian faith that we learn both what displeases God in the present and also what the new future is that God intends for the whole created order. But it is the preacher's task as well to view the world through the lens of those sacred texts and to discern and name what in the world is of God and what is not. To do so will require not only courage and wisdom but also imagination and love.

Cornel West's Definition

Finally, we turn to Cornel West, professor and scholar in the field of African American studies. While not specifically addressing the matter of prophetic *preaching*, West provides this provocative definition of prophetic *witness:*

> Prophetic witness consists of human acts of justice and kindness that attend to the unjust sources of human hurt and misery. Prophetic witness calls attention to the causes of unjustified suffering and unnecessary social misery. It highlights personal and institutional evil, including the evil of being indifferent to personal and institutional evil.[20]

West's definition adds at least two important insights to the conversation. First, he reminds us that prophetic witness is always bigger than preaching or the spoken word. Such witness also involves acts of justice and kindness and needs to go hand in hand with them. (I will speak more about the interplay between word and deed in prophetic witness in chapter 5.)

Second, West reminds us that prophetic witness focuses on both personal and institutional evil, "including the evil of being indifferent to personal and institutional evil." He continues, "The especial aim of prophetic utterance is to shatter deliberate ignorance and willful blindness to the suffering of others and to expose the clever forms of evasion and escape we devise in order to hide and conceal injustice. The prophetic goal is to stir up in us the courage to care and empower us to change our lives and our historical circumstances."[21]

SEVEN HALLMARKS OF PROPHETIC PREACHING

Ordinarily at this juncture the author of a book would state her own definition for prophetic preaching and argue why it is the best definition of all. But frankly, I think there is value in living within the tensions of the definitions offered by the scholars above and seeing the breadth of wisdom they corporately bring to us. While each definition certainly speaks to some aspect of prophetic preaching that is true and vitally important—be its biblical grounding, its social concern, its criticizing and energizing nature, or its imaginative calling—each definition also leaves out aspects of prophetic witness that are equally true and important. So rather than trying to provide a single definition that captures the entire essence of prophetic preaching, I prefer to identify some of the characteristics that make proclamation "prophetic." Here are seven hallmarks of prophetic preaching:

1. Prophetic preaching is rooted in the biblical witness: both in the testimony of the Hebrew prophets of old and in the words and deeds of the prophet Jesus of Nazareth.
2. Prophetic preaching is countercultural and challenges the status quo.
3. Prophetic preaching is concerned with the evils and shortcomings of the present social order and is often more focused on corporate and public issues than on individual and personal concerns.
4. Prophetic preaching requires the preacher to name both what is not of God in the world (criticizing) and the new reality God will bring to pass in the future (energizing).
5. Prophetic preaching offers hope of a new day to come and the promise of liberation to God's oppressed people.
6. Prophetic preaching incites courage in its hearers and empowers them to work to change the social order.
7. Prophetic proclamation requires of the preacher a heart that breaks with the things that break God's heart; a passion for justice in the world; the imagination, conviction, and courage to speak words from God; humility and honesty in the preaching moment; and a strong reliance on the presence and power of the Holy Spirit.

Having outlined the hallmarks of prophetic preaching, we now turn to the questions with which we began this chapter: Where have all the prophets gone? And why is it that so many pastors avoid or are fearful of becoming prophetic preachers themselves?

RESISTANCES TO PROPHETIC PREACHING

I indicated at the outset of this book that I have struggled throughout my ministry with how to become a faithful prophetic preacher, and that struggle has in large part led me to write this book. If I'm totally honest, I would have to admit that sometimes when I attempted to preach a "prophetic" sermon, I did so with a significant amount of anxiety and even downright fear. Prophetic preaching makes me nervous. It especially makes me nervous in contexts in which I feel that the message I am bringing is extremely countercultural.

I suspect that I am not alone in that anxiety. Indeed, as I talk with pastors around the country, I find many who believe that prophetic ministry is a part of their calling, but that doesn't mean they relish or look forward to it. And frankly, if they do look forward to it, that, too, is worrisome, for prophetic ministry—as best I can tell—is not one that the biblical prophets took on because they relished doing it; they did so only because God called them to it.

In the remainder of this chapter I will explore some of the reasons that pastors avoid or are fearful of becoming prophetic witnesses. I do not pretend that this list is exhaustive. Rather I am hopeful that it might "prime the pump" so that readers of this volume can begin naming and exploring some of their own resistances to prophetic witness.

1. An Inherited Model of Biblical Interpretation That Marginalizes the Prophetic Dimensions of Scripture

My own suspicion is that for some of us preachers (and my emphasis is definitely on the word "some") one challenge we face in claiming a rightful place for prophetic preaching is the marginalization the prophets and the prophetic dimensions of the gospel received in the churches of our own upbringings. Because some of us grew up in churches that thought politics had no place in the pulpit, that believed evangelism (not social justice) was at the heart and soul of the gospel of Christ, and that have, through their own biblical interpretation in preaching and teaching, relegated prophetic texts to the periphery of the Scriptures, we too have a tendency (even if a subconscious one) to place them there, too.

I grew up in a home where going to church and Sunday school, playing Bible Bee and Bible Bingo, and memorizing the Presbyterian catechisms on Sunday afternoons were the norm. I was an ace at Bible word drills and knew a lot of biblical trivia and a number of Scripture verses by memory by the time I left home to go to college. The churches of my youth held the Bible in high esteem and kindled within me a love for the Scriptures, for Jesus, and for the church.

But when I encountered the Hebrew prophets in college—under the tutelage of a Bible professor in a state university who made them come to life for me in that era of the Vietnam War, Watergate, and Kent State—it was as if I were hearing them for the very first time. Indeed, I think I *was* hearing some of them for the first time. And I remember wondering, Why is it that this whole, huge chunk of the Scriptures was underemphasized in my upbringing as a Christian in the church?

Now, I would like to think that in the intervening years, and especially given my own theological training and commitments, the tendency within me to marginalize the prophetic in the Scriptures has been handily checked. But what I find instead is that it still tends to raise its ugly head, despite my constant efforts to submerge it. This tendency especially manifests itself in an inclination to view biblical texts through the lens of personal piety and individual concerns more than through the lens of corporate and societal concerns.

For instance, it was not until I cotaught a course at Princeton Theological Seminary with my New Testament colleague Brian Blount on "Preaching the Gospel of Mark" that I began to see, really see as if for the first time, how highly prophetic Jesus' ministry in Mark's Gospel is. Frankly, I had always thought of Luke as the most "prophetic" of the Gospels and had seen Mark as a far tamer, even if firstborn, Synoptic cousin. But when Brian Blount interpreted those Markan texts about Jesus through the lens of his own African American church upbringing, he also opened my eyes to see a radical, boundary-breaking, world-upending Jesus for whom a prophetic preaching ministry was anything but optional! Indeed, what I learned through coteaching with Brian Blount is that if you try to cut the prophetic edge out of Jesus' proclamation in Mark, you've actually robbed this Gospel, and Jesus' very identity within it, of their heart and soul.[22]

For prophetic preaching to regain its rightful place as a central and not a peripheral act of Christian witness, I suspect that some of us will need to acknowledge that we need help in having the scales that have kept us from seeing the Bible itself as a highly prophetic book removed—not just once, but over and over again. And I also suspect that the churches, scholars, and preachers that will most help us in this endeavor are those who have long gravitated toward those prophetic texts because they have first heard them as Good News for the poor and oppressed, and not as bad news for the rich and powerful.

2. Pastoral Concern for Parishioners

Some of us preachers avoid preaching prophetically—or relegate such preaching to the margins—because we are, first and foremost, *pastors* who care passionately about our people, and we know that the last thing our parishioners need to hear is any more "bad news."

I returned to parish ministry seven years ago after spending over thirteen years in academia as a full-time seminary professor. I was poignantly reminded on my return of how deep and broad are the hurts and fears, the heartaches and disappointments, the illnesses and griefs and unfulfilled longings with which our people come to worship. It's no wonder pastors don't preach more prophetic sermons. For pastors rightly perceive that with prophetic preaching there is often bad news before there is good news. And the last thing we think our folk need is more bad news.

Walter Brueggemann readily acknowledges that the "criticizing" part of prophetic preaching often precedes the "energizing" part, and that such preaching can be difficult for hearers to embrace. But he also contends that "real criticism begins in the capacity to grieve because that is the most visceral announcement that things are not right."[23] The language the prophets of old used to criticize the old order was the language of grief or lament. As the prophet came to see the world through God's eyes, the prophet's own heart was broken by its injustice, inequality, and lack of peace. And the prophet shared that vision with a people who often did not want to be shaken out of their misperceptions of reality or told that the old order must die in order that a new might be born.

But Brueggemann also contends that "bringing hurt to public expression is an important first step in dismantling criticism that permits a new reality, theological and social, to emerge."[24] It is only as we recognize the necessity of the old order coming to an end—only as we lament and grieve its certain passing—that we can also be opened to God's *energizing* vision of a new order to come.

Yes, prophetic preaching does sometimes sound like bad news—especially for those who have a vested interest in preserving and protecting this world's unjust structures. But as Brueggemann reminds us, the bad news is never the ultimate word. It was through Good Friday that Easter and God's victory over evil arose. And it is through God's judgment of evil in our world and our church that God's healing grace, renewal, and restoration will also come.

3. Fear of Conflict

I think that some pastors avoid prophetic preaching because we minister in ecclesial contexts that are highly conflicted, and the last thing we want to do is add more fuel to the fires that already burn around us and that sometimes threaten to consume us.

It is no secret that today's church can be a highly conflicted place in which to minister. Churches are conflicted over doctrinal issues; over social and political issues; over ecclesial issues; and over countless petty issues. And sometimes they are even conflicted over what they should be most conflicted about! Those conflicts are sadly robbing some ministers of the joy of their vocation.

Several years ago I heard the pastor of a large church in New York City say that while he had no wish to relive the horrors of 9/11 and the tremendous toll it took on New Yorkers, he does sometimes grow nostalgic for the ministry he was able to do during the weeks after that event—in part because people had no time or energy for petty bickering. "I can't remember anyone," he said, "complaining about the bulletin announcements or the chair setups in their rooms on the Sundays following 9/11."

Pastors are understandably worn down, worn out, and distracted by the many conflicts that must be mediated in ministry these days, and thus it is partly for self-preservation that we avoid prophetic preaching. Mediating conflict takes an enormous amount of time and energy, and more conflict is not something most of us would take on voluntarily.

Having said that, I must also add that sometimes pastors may actually create more anxiety and conflict among their parishioners by not coming clean in the pulpit about where they stand on the critical issues of our day. A pastor recently told me that his congregation went through a difficult time several years ago when they rightly sensed that his own viewpoint on a critical issue before the church was shifting, but he was not forthcoming with them about it. His uncertainty led to a sense of insecurity as well as increased conflict on the part of his flock. He said that there was actually a sense of relief when he finally stated his own position forthrightly from the pulpit—even though a number of his parishioners strongly disagreed with him.

On the other hand, it is also important to acknowledge that pastors are human, and there may be seasons in our lives when self-care needs to be a priority in terms of our preaching agendas. I went through a battle with cancer in 2003 (from which I am now thankfully in remission), and during the early weeks after my diagnosis, I found that I simply could not tolerate any more bad or difficult news. I literally turned off the news when it came on. I also found that my energy was severely limited and that I needed to conserve most of it for the difficult task of healing. The last thing I needed was more conflict to mediate.

Many pastors have known seasons of illness, depression, burnout, anxiety, or despair during which they simply could not play the role of prophet as strongly as they might at other times because their own personal struggles were too great and too consuming. I think we need to acknowledge that in the ebb and flow of our own lives and in the lives of our congregations (who know their own share of ups and downs), there may well be "a time to plant, and a time to pluck up what is planted; . . . a time to break down, and a time to build up" (Eccl. 3:2b, 3b). Sometimes attending to the appropriate timing for prophetic witness from the pulpit is also important—for the pastor as well as for the congregation.

4. Fear of Dividing a Congregation

Given the already conflicted realities of congregations these days, one of the things pastors fear most in prophetic preaching is having their own congregations torn asunder by their preaching. One pastor friend described the current situation in this way:

> Our nation is so polarized ideologically that even to name prophetic topics in the pulpit causes people's defenses immediately to go up. It is as if the media pundits have stolen those topics from the church and politicized them. Rush Limbaugh got to the issues first. So there is no such thing as a blank slate upon which to make a reasoned argument. Consequently people either turn you off or go immediately to their own positions as soon as you mention an issue. It's hard to make a case that a prophetic concern is really a spiritual or religious issue.

People come to church, this pastor contended, because they hunger for a place of belonging that is not as divided as our nation is. They hunger for a sense of unity and purpose. And the last thing they want is a church that is as divided as the rest of society.

While it is certainly true that prophetic witness can lead to division in a congregation (after all, even Jesus said that he came not "to bring peace, but a sword"[Matt. 10:34], and history has clearly evidenced the fact that not everyone will readily embrace such witness), it is also true that conversations around divisive issues, if undertaken in a spirit of Christian compassion and openness, can lead people in Christian communities to a deeper understanding of one another and the reasons they differ.

In her book *Caretakers of Our Common House*, Christian educator Carol Lakey Hess argues for what she calls "hard dialogue and deep connections"[25] in faith communities. Hard dialogue engages in "real talk": talk that is "collaborative, mutual, and deeply inter- and intra-personal. . . . Real talk is empathetic, nonjudgmental, and receptive; and yet it is also passionate, honest and self-disclosing."[26] Such dialogue, Hess contends, "will enable communities to 'go deep.' Inviting all to participate as knowers, integrating personal feelings and life experience into abstract reflection, and calling for the disciplines of listening to and understanding one another—real talk is both hard and deep."[27]

This is the kind of dialogue the members of the Theological Task Force on Peace, Unity, and Purity of my own denomination undertook several years ago when a diverse group of Presbyterians came together for two years to discuss our denomination's stand regarding the ordination of gays and lesbians.[28] By beginning their meetings with prayer and Bible study, the committee found common ground from which to discuss their differences as well as share the life experiences that had helped shape their varied perspectives. Miraculously, they also came to consensus and unanimously adopted the report they presented to our church. While not everyone agreed with the task force's proposals, it was readily apparent that the Spirit had been at work in their midst and that this group of Christians were no longer strangers, shooting at one another from opposite sides of the divide, but had become respectful friends.

Conflict, we need to be reminded, can have positive as well as negative effects in the life of Christian communities. Indeed, sometimes conversions take place and lifelong friendships are forged across lines of difference when people are willing to risk entering with one another into "hard dialogue."

5. Fear of Being Disliked, Rejected, or Made to Pay a Price for Prophetic Witness

Several years ago I led a workshop on prophetic preaching for an ecumenical gathering of pastors in New Hampshire. At the midday break one of the participants came up to me—a man who had been in ministry for many years and was nearing retirement—and spoke with me about his own fears. "I want to be honest here and say that I am afraid to be a prophetic preacher. I need my job. I am the sole support of my family, and I need my income to support us. When I read what happened to the prophets of old, and the price they often paid for their witness, it terrifies me. I simply cannot afford to pay such a price."

For most pastors I know (including myself), fear lies at the heart of our resistance to bearing prophetic witness—fear of not being liked, fear of rejection, fear of being attacked by those who disagree with us, fear of not being able to adequately defend our point of view, or even fear of losing our jobs. We may also be afraid of damaging our pastoral relationship with our flock or making those we love pay a high price for our prophetic words and actions.

In her book *Transforming the Stone,* Barbara Lundblad contends that fear is often at the root of parishioners' resistances to prophetic preaching as well. People fear change and the things it might require of them. But Lundblad reminds us that fears do not go away if we sweep them under the rug and refuse to talk about them. It is only as we begin to name them—honestly and forthrightly—and acknowledge the hold they have over our lives that we are able to take the first step toward moving beyond fear to faith and to embracing the whole gospel God has entrusted to us.[29]

I think the time has come for pastors to begin honestly naming their fears—as the pastor who approached me that day in New Hampshire did. Sometimes it is when we are willing to go to the depths of our fears and envision the worst that might happen to us—facing those demons squarely in the face—that we also begin to find the God-given power to confront and exorcise them.

Theologian Scott Bader-Saye reminds us that courage is not the absence of fear. Rather "courage is the capacity to do what is right and good in the face of fear. We become courageous when we learn to live for something that is more important than our own safety."[30] Bader-Saye continues:

The courageous person feels fear but is not overcome by it. The courageous person recognizes danger but refuses to let fear get in the way of doing what is right, good, and necessary. The courageous person also shows prudence in the face of danger, since prudence (or "practical wisdom") is an important companion virtue to courage.[31]

By honestly naming our own fears before God and others, we also open ourselves to the Holy Spirit, who alone can give us the courage we need to confront and act in the midst of our fears.

6. Feelings of Inadequacy in Addressing Prophetic Concerns

There used to be a time in our country's life when pastors were among the most educated persons in their communities and when general knowledge was more prevalent than specialized knowledge. But such is no longer the case. Pastors increasingly find themselves addressing issues from the pulpit on which they are not nearly as well versed as some of their congregants, and consequently, they can feel woefully inadequate in even attempting to do so.

How do you preach on issues of economic justice when a professor of economics is one of your congregants? How do you preach on genetic engineering when there are within your congregation biologists and medical personnel who know far more about its intricacies than you can pretend to know? Even if the specialists are not actually within the congregation, most pastors are wise enough to acknowledge that they know very little about a lot of things—and consequently they wonder how, in the course of an ordinary week of sermon preparation, they can possibly address the complex issues of our day without looking like fools.

Certainly a word can be said at this point about the wisdom of doing one's homework before preaching on prophetic issues. I am told that William Sloane Coffin spent about six months studying a controversial topic, immersing himself in arguments on all sides of the issue, before he preached on it. Some prophetic issues deserve to be undergirded by serious study and reflection before they are brought into the pulpit.

And certainly a word can be said about the need for humility in prophetic preaching and the wisdom of approaching people in the congregation who have more knowledge than we on particular issues and asking them to help educate us. All of this is well and good.

But it is also important that the preacher realize that she or he does have particular expertise—*theological* expertise—that can be shared from the pulpit, and that often what people hunger for when they come to church is some word from God that addresses the concerns of their day. Parishioners do not want the preacher to be another political pundit, another talk show expert, or another scientist arguing her case. What they long for is what I longed for in my hometown during those days of serious racial tension and upheaval: someone who, with intelligence and compassion and courage, will stand in the pulpit and help them think differently about what it means to approach the world in which they live as a Christian—and how, as Christians, they might believe and live differently in light of what the Scriptures teach. To carry out this task does not require new expertise as much as it requires a willingness to think deeply and long about the burning issues of our day, and the courage to address them from the pulpit.

7. Discouragement That Our Own Prophetic Witness Is Not Making a Difference

Finally, I think we need to acknowledge that some of us avoid prophetic preaching because we have tried to be faithful in preaching this way and have ended up discouraged, frustrated, and even defeated by the responses we have received.

Ethicist James Childs shares this telling story about pastors and their frustrations in prophetic preaching:

Not long ago I was discussing with a group of pastors issues of economic justice from the perspective of a Christian ethic. The response of several was not entirely surprising. "This is all well and good," they said, "but the world in which we live doesn't know and doesn't care about this stuff. We're in a very different place." They were discouraged and frustrated. They saw themselves being dismissed by the world around them as irrelevant, relegated to the role of shamans in a ghetto of personal spirituality.

Such feelings and fears, which are not new, often lead to either resignation or attack, neither of which is helpful. On the one hand, some persons in ministry accept what they consider to be the judgment of the world around them and slip into the safety of quietism. On the other hand, those who attack shake their fists at an unjust world in a cascade of condemnations. They are determined to be prophetic. Like so many journalistic social critics without a proposal who expose our underside with acerbic eloquence, they finally become tiresome. Despite the contrast in responses, they share with their quietistic colleagues a common conviction that work for justice and the common good in this world is futile.[32]

My own suspicion is that prophets rarely know the difference they are making at the time they speak. Indeed, since the first response to prophetic speech is often resistance, resistance is all they may experience. But prophetic ministry—like other forms of ministry—is often about planting seeds that, in God's good timing, may well bear fruit.

I once heard a seminary professor tell about being a parish pastor in Arkansas back in the 1960s and taking a strong stand for civil rights that many people in the congregation opposed. Someone even wrote a letter to the editor of the local newspaper suggesting that he should leave town immediately. Years later he was invited back to preach for an anniversary celebration at that church, and he was absolutely amazed by how many people—including a number of those who had opposed him at the time—lined up outside the church to thank him for his witness in their midst.

We are called to be faithful in ministry, not successful, so if we measure the fruits of prophetic witness by results that we can see, we are very likely to be disappointed. But if we trust the fruits to God, who knows what harvest may be born of our labors?

CONCLUSION

If truth be told, pastors avoid prophetic witness for many reasons, and not all of them are altogether wrongheaded. Pastors should care about the effect their words will have on their congregants. They should be concerned about maintaining some sort of balance between the prophetic and the pastoral in their ministries. And they should attend to their own self-care, especially during times when their physical or mental health is on the line.

But I am also convinced that much of what lies at the malaise over prophetic preaching in our day—whether it issues in quietism or in condemnation on the part of the preacher—is a spiritual problem. *We have lost our will to preach prophetically because we have lost the prophetic vision that comes from being intimately connected with God, with God's world, and with God's people.* And so in the next chapter I want to talk about reconnections we can make in our lives of faith that can go a long way toward rekindling within us a renewed passion for prophetic ministry.

2

Rekindling the Fire Within:
A Spirituality for Prophetic Witness

If our sermons are to revive the social gospel, if our homilies are to inspire as well as inform, our preachers must be set aflame. Not just provided with information, data, skills, strategies, important as these are. Even more importantly, a spirituality; in fact, a conversion that turns the preacher inside out, puts "fire in the belly."[1]

Walter J. Burghardt, SJ, *Preaching the Just Word*

Only those who come to see the world as God sees the world, only those who see through the eyes of God, ever really see the glory of the world, ever really approach the peaceable kingdom, ever find peace in themselves.[2]

Joan D. Chittister, OSB, *There Is a Season*

Several years ago I attended an event where a Christian laywoman, who was also her state's commissioner for education, addressed a group of pastors and seminary professors of my denomination. "What has happened to our church?" she asked us. "Back in the sixties we had a fire in our bellies. We cared passionately about civil rights, the war in Vietnam, and other issues of our day. Some of us even put our own bodies on the line for causes we believed in, boarding buses for freedom rides, or marching in the streets. Where have the fires of our passion gone?"

While I do not want to glorify the sixties (for it was a very complex time) or my denomination's prophetic witness during that period (for if truth be told, it was only a remnant who had that "fire in their bellies"), I do believe that the fires of prophetic witness are burning dimly these days and in some instances are in danger of being extinguished altogether.

At root, this malaise is a spiritual problem. For it is the Spirit of God, according to the Scriptures, who gives the prophet not only a call but also the message to deliver and the passion and courage to deliver it. If the flames of prophetic passion are to be rekindled, it is the Spirit who will need to relight them.

Sadly, however, the church itself often contributes to the prophetic torpor of our time by creating divides between things that should be united. One of the most troubling divides is between practices of spirituality (such as prayer, devotional reading of Scriptures, and meditation), on the one hand, and social activism and action in the public realm, on the other. All too often churches line up on either side of the divide, with congregations either offering parishioners a place where they can love Jesus with their whole hearts and practice a warmhearted piety (thus focusing on the internal life of the Christian), or a place where they can discern God's activity in the world and become passionate about social justice (focusing on the external life of faith). I am convinced that until we get these two aspects of Christian discipleship back together again and in some semblance of balance in our churches, neither our spirituality nor our activism will be all that it could be.

Social activists need to be deeply rooted in spiritual practices so that they can discern where it is that God is calling them to speak and to act in the world, and so that they can tap into the power of the Holy Spirit, which is much bigger and greater than our own. Pietists, on the other hand, need to get out of their prayer closets and into the larger world in order to discover the fullness of the God whose face is often most clearly revealed to us in the face of the poor, the outcast, and the marginalized.

What we Christians need today is what James Forbes, retired pastor of Riverside Church in New York City, calls "a spirituality for activism"[3]: a spirituality that can undergird, empower, and sustain us in our prophetic witness in the world.

In the remainder of this chapter I will outline what such a spirituality might look like for contemporary believers. I will identify other disconnects in our lives as Christians that feed our resistance to prophetic witness and also reflect on how we might reconnect them. In the process I hope to bring to the fore a spirituality that honors head and heart; inner life and outer witness: and listening, speaking, and doing.

RECLAIMING A SPIRITUALITY FOR ACTIVISM

1. Reconnecting the Life of Solitude (Silence) and the Gift of Prophetic Speech

Joan Chittister is a Roman Catholic sister of the Benedictine order who has become, in recent years, an outspoken and eloquent prophet regarding many dimensions of our national life. Her writings evoke a rare blend of bold, prophetic truth speaking and a disciplined life of prayer, meditation, and reflection.

In her book *There Is a Season*, structured around the different seasons mentioned in the Ecclesiastes text that begins, "For everything there is a season, and a time for every matter under heaven" (Eccl. 3:1), Chittister includes these words in her chapter titled "A Time for Peace":

> There are some things in life that deserve to be nourished simply for their own sake. Art is one, music is another, good reading is a third, but the power of the contemplative vision is the greatest of them all. Only those who come to see the world as God sees the world, only those who see through the eyes of God, ever really see the glory of the world, ever really approach the peaceable kingdom, ever find peace in themselves.[4]

Silence, Chittister says, is the beginning of peace. But silence is also an endangered species in our time. In a previous era, she says,

> silence was a given. Men went with the flocks up a lonely mountain for weeks and had to learn to be at peace with themselves. Women worked in the kitchens of the world grinding corn and plucking chickens, deep in thought, attuned to the things around them. Children picked in the fields in long, separated rows, learning young to hear birds and wind and water, weaving their fancies from the materials of the earth. Silence was a friendly part of life, not a deprivation, not a fearsome place to be.[5]

Chittister's writing evokes memories of the long periods of silence I would have as a child while shelling peas with my grandmother on a summer's day, or while walking home alone from my weekly piano lessons and inventing stories in my head. In the days before iPods, Blackberries, and cell phones, silence was a natural part of the rhythm of everyday life. But now I fear that it is increasingly becoming an endangered species.

Chittister says that if we're ever going to regain peace in our own souls and an ability to listen deeply to God, we have to recover silence. Without it, the prophetic vision of a world at peace will surely die.

The Witness of the Riverside Preachers

I spent three years of my scholarly life researching and writing about the preachers of The Riverside Church in New York City, a church that has given a highly prophetic witness in this nation since its founding in 1930. One of the things that has both intrigued me and also distressed me in my reading about the early Riverside preachers is how much of the day the early preachers there spent in silence—and how much of that silence has been lost for preachers today.

Harry Emerson Fosdick, the first and perhaps most famous of the Riverside preachers, spent each weekday morning—from his rising until lunchtime—sequestered in his study, where he prayed, contemplated, read the Bible and other books, and prepared for his preaching and teaching engagements. Out of that silence flowed the powerful sermons Fosdick preached at Riverside each week—sermons that were also heard by thousands of listeners around the world who tuned in each Sunday afternoon to the *National Vespers* radio program. Fosdick also used that time to prepare the Wednesday night lectures he regularly gave at the church—many of which were later published in books he also wrote during his ministry (fifty in total!). Fosdick largely left the day-to-day programmatic and administrative running of the church to the laity, which freed him for the primary tasks of pastoral ministry: preaching, teaching, and pastoral care. And when he charged his successor at Riverside, Robert James McCracken, at McCracken's service of installation, he did so with these words:

> Welcome to this church. It is a seven-day-a-week affair with more things going on here than you can possibly keep track of. Don't try to. Most of all we want your message in the pulpit, born out of long hours of study, meditation and prayer. Guard your morning privacy as a sacred trust![6]

It was clearly silence that fed the greatness of Fosdick's preaching and teaching, as well as that of his successor at Riverside, Jim McCracken. Yet sadly, most pastors I know have precious little of it in the course of their work week. Somehow we have allowed the day-to-day administration of the church, constant pastoral needs, and endless interruptions to usurp its place. And the result is not only clergy burnout but also a lack of visionary, prophetic leadership in the pulpit. In order to regain such a vision, Fosdick would suggest, we need to claim a place for silence in our lives—silence in which we listen for the voice of God—and allow that silence to be at the center of all that we do and say.

The Quakers

Silence also plays a major role in the prophetic witness of the Quakers. My daughter attended Guilford College, a small Quaker college in

Greensboro, North Carolina, that is profiled in the book *Colleges That Change Lives.*[7] For her it was the perfect fit, encouraging and nourishing the activism for peace and justice that was already a part of her viscera. Her sojourn there also allowed our family an opportunity to become better acquainted with the Quakers.

One of the things that fascinates me about the Quakers is the way their silence in worship and their prophetic witness in the world go hand in hand. The Quakers were among the first Christian traditions to advocate the abolition of slavery, the right of women to vote, and a pacifist stance in times of war. For those stands, they have frequently been ridiculed and sometimes persecuted. While a highly verbal Presbyterian like me would suspect that such activism would surely have been born out of good, solid, biblical preaching, the truth is that it wasn't. Quite the opposite. It was born out of silence. A silence in which good Quakers sit—sometimes for hours—waiting for the Spirit to reveal the things of God to them.

If we are going to regain a passion for prophetic witness, I suspect we have a lot to learn from the Quakers and from the early Riverside preachers. For it is only as we allow time for silence and for the unhindered movement of God's Spirit in its midst that a new vision for God's world is likely to emerge.

2. Reconnecting Our Lives and the Lives of Those Who Are Suffering

No matter what we say about prophetic witness, I am convinced that one of the chief spiritual motivators for us will always be our own first-hand involvement with people who are suffering. That is why international mission trips, inner-city tutoring programs, volunteer work in homeless shelters, serving meals in soup kitchens, and building homes for Habitat for Humanity are such important activities for us as Christians. Not so much because we give to others through those activities— important as that may be—but because when we step out of our own comfort zones and our own safe neighborhoods and secure homes and hang out with the people Jesus hung out with, it changes us. When we listen to their stories, witness their struggles, and also glimpse their courage, faith, and generosity in the midst of it all, we become more aware of the systemic problems that contribute to their plight—and our attitudes toward those problems change.

Rick Ufford-Chase, a Presbyterian elder who has devoted much of his life to ministry on behalf of immigrants who are fleeing Central America to come to the United States, preached a sermon during his year as Moderator of the Presbyterian Church (U.S.A.) General Assembly in which he urged his hearers to become more involved in justice ministries in the world.[8] He said he had once been to a conference at which Gustavo Gutiérrez was invited to be the keynote speaker. At the last minute, Gutiérrez's visa was denied, so Robert McAfee Brown agreed to step in for him. McAfee Brown told about being at a lecture Gutiérrez had given and hearing Gutiérrez say—in response to a question about how Christians of privilege and power should live more faithfully—that it would take at least three things for Christians to move from inertia to prophetic action in the public arena:

> First, that each of us be willing to spend time personally with people who are living on the margins of society, so that we can listen to their stories, hear their frustrations, and open ourselves to their anger and despair and pain—and not just do so by proxy (by sending money, food, or supplies). He also insisted that this contact must be regular and consistent, leading to the establishment of personal relationships.
>
> Second, that each one of us be willing to use the power that we have in becoming advocates for those people God lays on our hearts, . . .
>
> And third (and this is the hardest part, he said), that we also risk giving up some of our own privilege, so that others may receive what is just and right and good for them.[9]

When I think of people I know who have engaged in prophetic witness in the world, this is the path many of them have taken. They begin with firsthand interaction with and concern for a marginalized people—often through volunteer work. They then gain a willingness to become vocal advocates in the public arena for the larger (and often more systemic) issues and concerns raised through that firsthand engagement. And finally they reexamine their own lives and ask what they might be required to sacrifice for the sake of a greater good for all.

The fact that the journey begins in a small way should not be underestimated. For it is often through that firsthand encounter with the other and a mutual sharing of life stories that a person's entire worldview begins to change, and she or he begins to sense the Spirit's prompting. Thus, it is critically important that the church not draw too strong a dividing line between hands-on mission and justice advocacy. Both are needed, and quite often it is the firsthand engagement with people who are suffering that lights the flames of passion for advocacy.

Fifth Avenue Presbyterian Church

I served for four years on the staff of Fifth Avenue Presbyterian Church in New York City, a church that in recent decades has ministered to and with the homeless population of that city. For a number of years homeless people have slept both in the shelter inside the church and on the front steps. Through the years members of the congregation have come to know these homeless folk as friends, and the church regularly hosts events that bring the homeless and the church members together for meals and fellowship.

Back in the 1990s Mayor Rudy Giuliani mounted a campaign to "clean up" New York and to make the city a safer and more attractive place for tourists. In the process, his administration threatened to arrest any of the homeless who were found sleeping on the front steps of buildings along Fifth Avenue—including church buildings. When that threat became real for Fifth Avenue Church, the officers moved from being friends of the homeless to becoming their advocates. They went outside and placed tape all along the sidewalk that borders the church's building at the corner of Fifth Avenue and 55th Street. They then told city officials that the part of the city on the street side of that tape rightly belonged to the city, and they could do as they pleased with it. But located on the other side of the tape was the house of God, and in God's house, all—and especially the homeless—were welcome.

The church doggedly refused to allow the city to arrest the homeless who slept on its steps, and the city subsequently sued the church for its defiance of their demands. The case went all the way to the state supreme court, with the church being vindicated at each stage of the process and ultimately winning its case. Needless to say, the lawsuit cost the church a great deal in terms of time, personnel, and money—but the price was clearly well worth it.

When pastors and congregations get involved in a personal way with those who are poor or oppressed, the journey toward justice begins. It may take a while for people to move from firsthand involvement to advocacy, and then to a willingness to sacrifice for the cause, but the first step is clearly a critical one. In addition, as many who have been involved in such ministries will readily testify, the spiritual benefits—in terms of deepened understandings of faith and faithfulness—are incalculable.

3. Reconnecting the Individual and the Social/ Corporate Worlds in Biblical Interpretation

In the last chapter I suggested that some pastors resist prophetic preaching because they grew up in churches that did not give enough attention to the prophetic dimensions of Scripture. The Bible was read through an individualistic and pietistic lens, and consequently its more corporate and prophetic witness was silenced. Unfortunately, this trend still continues today in churches where participants in Christian education classes are encouraged to think more about what a biblical text means for them individually and personally than about what it might mean for the larger society, nation, or world.

Social ethicist Dieter Hessel has suggested that if preaching is to become more socially transformative, interpreters of the Scriptures must develop a social hermeneutic for its interpretation. "Of particular interest here," he says, "is a method of interpretation which makes clear the liberating meaning of Biblical texts for human-social existence today."[10] Hessel encourages leaders of Bible study groups not only to ask participants for a "personal-private" interpretation of a biblical text but also to ask them for a "social-corporate" interpretation.[11] He provides the following example of interpretations offered by a Bible study group while engaging in the study of 1 Corinthians 1:18–21 (a text about "God's Foolish Wisdom") back in the 1980s:

Personal-Private Meanings

I boast in the Lord who saved me. The cross of Christ exposes my sin. I can withdraw from worldly struggle; God is on my side. God favors sinners; salvation is in the cross.

Social-Corporate Meanings

Christ upset the existing order for the sake of the lowly. Christians reject ideological justifications for corporate wealth and military policy. A power-made and success-oriented society ignores the humanizing power of the cross. Is high technology wise? Is denuclearization foolish? Our common human weakness and social sin is the bond of humility and compassion.[12]

I wonder what would happen if preachers, in the midst of preparing their sermons, followed Hessel's model for biblical interpretation. What if instead of asking either about the personal implications of a text or about a text's sociocultural meanings, pastors asked about *both*.

As I am writing this chapter I am also undertaking Bible study for the sake of a sermon I will preach on Palm/Passion Sunday based on Mark 11:1–11. As I ask these questions regarding that familiar Palm Sunday text, I come up with my own two interpretations:

Personal-Private Meanings

Jesus is the celebrity I greet, along with the crowds, with joy and admiration on Palm Sunday. I want his autograph, I am awed to be in his presence, and I am happy to wave my own palm branch to welcome him to town. But alas, before week's end my sins and silences will have crucified him. What a bittersweet day this is—for me and for him. My heart rejoices in his advent, even as it breaks over how this week will surely end.

Social-Corporate Meanings

The religious community expects a messiah after the order of David, riding on a stallion, and instead they get a peacemaker riding on a colt. The city expects a guest, grateful for its adulation and exuberant welcome, and instead they got a prophet who tells them that the temple must fall because it (like the fig tree) is not bearing fruit. I wonder what critiques Jesus would make of us today: As a city? As a nation? As a religious people? What injustices in our past would he name as he seeks to prune us? What would he say about our current social order that would cause us, like the crowd at Jerusalem, to turn on him, and demand his death?

4. Reconnecting the Pastoral and the Prophetic in Ministry

In homiletical literature, "pastoral" preaching and "prophetic" preaching are often defined as if they are two separate and distinct entities. For instance, J. Randall Nichols defines *prophetic preaching* as "preaching about God's being and activity, directing our attention to the mission of Christian faith and action in a desperate world, and calling on the church as organic entity to find itself and respond." *Priestly preaching*, on the other hand, "means preaching about human brokenness and travail, directing us to the need for inner renewal and strength, addressing us as individual children of God being sought by a Lord who loves us as he does every sparrow that falls."[13]

However, rather than seeing these two options as posing a choice for the preacher, Nichols urges us to see them as two ends of a dialectical spectrum that keeps preaching in balance. As he puts it, the tension posed "is not a 'conflict' to be 'resolved' but a dynamic interaction to be sustained."[14] The wise pastor lives within that dynamic tension, recognizing that many individual sermons—and the trajectory of sermons over the long term—will have elements of both poles within them. Indeed, Nichols argues that "*if we should by chance succeed in preaching wholly on one side or the other, we would so distort reality as to foreclose the communicative work of the very things we wish to cultivate.*"[15]

While this book is certainly calling for a renewed interest in the prophetic dimensions of preaching (since, in my view, the pendulum has swung too far toward the pastoral end of the spectrum), I am also aware that these two aspects of ministry are integrally related. Indeed, prophetic preaching often depends on pastoral ministry for its impetus, its context, and its follow-up care. Furthermore, prophetic preaching can often initiate a conversation that continues pastorally long after the sermon has ended.

Harry Emerson Fosdick, the founding pastor of The Riverside Church, is an interesting case study in prophetic preaching because Fosdick was a prophet not in spite of the fact that he was a pastor but precisely *because* he was a pastor. The more deeply Fosdick came to know his flock—not only the flock that packed The Riverside Church sanctuary each week to listen to his sermons but also the flock around the world to whom he ministered through his *National Vespers* radio program—the more he became aware of their suffering. And it was ultimately his pastor's heart that led him to become a prophet.

Fosdick is probably best known for two courageous stands that he took during his ministry: his "modernist" stance theologically in the midst of the fundamentalist-modernist theological debates that rocked this country in the early twentieth century (and which are still very much alive in some sectors of the church today), and his pacifist stance in relation to war, a stance he maintained throughout World War II.

Yet what is interesting to me about Fosdick's story is that he was not always a pacifist. Indeed, he was highly supportive of World War I and traveled to Europe to spend several months ministering to the troops on the front lines of that war, urging them on with his prayers and his hymns. But that experience of war and his pastoral care of soldiers in its midst also changed Fosdick in a major way. When he saw firsthand what war did to people—not only to those civilians who were caught in its crossfire but also to those soldiers that he sent off to battle with a hymn and a prayer, he did a complete about-face. He ended up preaching a sermon on the day when the Tomb of the Unknown Soldier was being dedicated all over the world. It is one of the most eloquent defenses of pacifism I have ever heard.[16]

But it is also important to know that while Fosdick regularly preached pacifism from The Riverside Church pulpit during World War II, he also reached out pastorally to the men and women of the armed services who worshiped at Riverside. Every Sunday, beginning the Sunday following the bombing of Pearl Harbor, the worship bulletin at Riverside Church included a notice telling service men and women that if they would let Dr. Fosdick know of their presence in church that day, he would send a handwritten letter to their family back home, telling them of their loved one's presence in worship. During those same years, on Sunday afternoons, Riverside Church became the regular worship space for the Navy Midshipmen's School, and many service men and women were married in its chapel or sanctuary.[17]

Frankly, I learn some things from Fosdick's witness about what a Christian spirituality for activism looks like. First, Fosdick's brand of spirituality reminds me that it is possible to advocate strongly for a cause without at the same time condemning those who disagree with you. He also shows me that it is possible to speak up boldly for peace without at the same time condemning those who are caught up in the complexities of war. In short, Fosdick models how to be prophetic while also being hospitable.

Pastoral Follow-up to Prophetic Witness

A pastor of a small church in the Northeast, who was attending a continuing education event I was leading, told a moving story about her own attempt to reconnect the pastoral and the prophetic in parish ministry. She said that her seminary intern preached one Sunday on a highly controversial justice topic and that on the way out of worship, a man who had been regularly visiting with her congregation took off his name tag, tore it in tiny pieces, threw them on the floor at her (the pastor's) feet, and announced that after that sermon, he would never return to the church again.

The pastor recounted how she was deeply troubled by this incident and prayed for wisdom about how to respond pastorally without also undercutting her intern's witness. She took the pieces of the name tag to her office and kept them in a bowl because she simply couldn't let them (or him) go. Finally, she decided on a course of action. With painstaking care she put the pieces of the name tag back together with tape and sent them to the man by mail with a handwritten note. In it she told him that she was glad he had visited her congregation, that she was sorry the sermon had been so upsetting to him, and that her door was always open to him if he wanted to talk further about the sermon. She also told him that the church would gladly welcome him back if at any time he wanted to return.

A spirituality for activism will recognize that the pastoral and the prophetic are not altogether separate but are often two sides of the same coin. We are called to be prophetic in part because, like Fosdick, we are pastors who care about everything that impinges on the lives of our parishioners. Yet we are also called to remember that pastoral care not only precedes but also follows prophetic witness. And sometimes the proof that we are speaking truth "in love" is our willingness to care deeply for those who disagree with us.

5. Reconnecting Prayer and Prophetic Witness

One of the things I most appreciated about my sojourn on the pastoral staff of Fifth Avenue Presbyterian Church in New York City was the seriousness with which that congregation took prayer. This was a body of believers who prayed regularly, faithfully, and nonperfunctorily.

Each Sunday before the two morning worship services, church officers would gather with the pastors in the vestry for a circle of prayer before the service. They offered prayers for the sick and grieving, for the victims of the latest natural disaster in our world, for homeless friends in the city (a number of whom slept in our shelter or on our front steps), and also for the morning worship service. After worship, Stephen Ministers and deacons were available in the front of our sanctuary for one-on-one confidential prayer with anyone who needed it. And at least once a quarter people had an opportunity to attend a special afternoon service in the chapel where prayers were offered for "healing and peace."

Frankly, I am convinced that if congregations and other faith-based communities today are going to join in prophetic witness, that witness will need to arise out of prayer: prayer of the preacher, prayer of church leaders, and prayer of the congregation. And there are at least three types of prayer that need to be reclaimed and reconnected with the church's prophetic mission: (1) prayer in which we seek discernment for the particular witness God would have us make; (2) prayer in which we are honest with God about our fears, our differences, and our struggles; and (3) prayer in which we regain the ability to lament and to mourn before God the brokenness of our world.

Prayers of Discernment

A pastor of a large predominantly Euro-American church in New York City told me that soon after he came to the city, he received some very sage advice from the pastor of a large predominantly African American congregation that was genuinely making a difference in the city. The African American pastor told him, "Whatever you do in advocacy or mission in this city, go deep in one area or one issue. Don't try to respond to every need of this city; there are too many of them. Rather, concentrate on the one thing God would have you and your congregation do and do well, and dig a deep well of witness there." "And frankly," this wise pastor continued, "if you're in prayer to God about what that one thing might be for you, it will most likely come to you. You won't have to go out looking for it."

I think that is sage advice for all congregations, wherever and whatever our witness may be. If we think that to be prophetic we have to offer our opinion or engage in action on every issue that comes down the pike, we will dilute our witness and also wear ourselves out. But if we focus our primary energies on going deep in one area or two—whether it be hunger or homelessness or war and peace or labor rights or care for immigrants or prison ministry or bolstering inner-city schools—we will find that we not only strengthen our prophetic witness but also are able to engage the gifts and talents of a variety of congregation members who can join the cause on different levels and in different ways. But the first step is to be in serious prayer together about where our primary witness should lie, where God's Spirit would lead us to dig deep wells of witness.

Prayers of Honest Confession

In her book *Transforming the Stone*, Barbara Lundblad rightly notes that the resistance to prophetic witness is often born out of fear.

> As we look around the landscape of our country and the larger world, we need to acknowledge that many, including ourselves, are scrambling to secure a place, to shore up the shifting sands:
> *Shore up the borders!* Build a barrier to keep out immigrants (at least those we don't want).
> *Shore up the streets!* Remove the homeless from our neighborhoods. Make us safer by legalizing the death penalty.
> *Shore up the family!* Pass the "Defense of Marriage Act" to protect traditional values.
> *Shore up the church!* Return to tradition. Silence the voice of feminists. Get back to the Bible.[18]

Lundblad believes that "if we listen carefully to the words and the emotions behind the words we hear a great deal of fear."[19] And since "calls for radical change [through prophetic preaching] may only increase the uncertainty many are experiencing, . . . our response [as preachers] is to try to avoid fearful changes: keep things the way they are, sing the familiar hymns, stay clear of shifting sand."[20]

The problem, Lundblad says, is that even if we succeed in avoiding all conflict and controversy, the fears won't go away. *It is only by naming them*, by boldly addressing them, by bringing a new word from the Lord to bear in the face of them, that the church's witness can become genuinely transformative.

If the church is going to become faithful in prophetic witness, we need to become bolder about acknowledging to God and to one another our fears, our resistances, and the places where we disagree. And we also need to pray with and for one another, so that whether in the end we agree to stay together or to part ways, we do not lose sight of one another as beloved children of God.

Prayers of Mourning and Lament

One of the things I love about worshiping with people who have been through hard times—who have suffered from addictions or spent time in prison or lived on the streets—is the honesty of their prayers. These believers don't tend to clean up their prayers, or try to make them pretty. Instead, what often emerge in communal prayer are the deepest laments of the human soul: laments over sin and its consequences in our lives, and laments over structures that are not as just as God would have them be in our society.

If the church is going to care as passionately about the world as God does, we will need to reclaim the ability to lament in our prayers: to lament over that in our own lives which is sinful and not of God; to lament over that in our city and nation which is sinful and not of God; and to lament over that in the world which is sinful and not of God. We will need to allow our own hearts to break over the things that break God's heart. For with a broken heart our eyes are more able to see the world as God sees it.

If we will regain such prayer—in all its honesty and transforming power—I am convinced that God will also lead us into areas of vital prophetic witness. For such witness reflects the heart of God's only Son who loved this entire world so very much that he wept over Jerusalem and took all of this world's suffering upon himself on a cross.

6. Reconnecting Individuals and Communities in Prophetic Witness

In his book *Following Jesus in a Culture of Fear,* theologian Scott Bader-Saye writes, "Courage requires community, both for the learning of courage and the living of it."[21] Such is certainly the case with prophetic witness. We learn courage for prophetic witness by our life in Christian community, where we read about the bold actions of the prophets of biblical times, are moved by the witness of the saints and martyrs throughout church history, and come face to face with contemporary saints whose witness for Christ inspires our own.

Yet Christian community is also the place where we find the ongoing courage for the living of our lives in prophetic witness here and now. As any would-be prophet knows, it is easy to have the fires of our ardor turn to ash if they are not rekindled by the prayers and hymns of the faithful. It is easy to have our resolve turn to fear if we are not surrounded by those believers who make us want to become our best selves in Christ. And it is easy to think that we are the crazy ones in this out-of-kilter world if we are not continually reminded that the ways of God are frequently countercultural, and that there are others in the Christian community who share our views and values.

Certainly not all Christian congregations offer the kind of community that supports prophetic witness. As Bader-Saye rightly reminds us, "Over time a church can settle into patterns of institutional life that turn the focus inward and tempt a people to become content with self-preservation. Some have called such communities 'maintenance churches.'"[22] Pastors ministering within maintenance churches may well need to look outside the bounds of their congregations—and perhaps outside the bounds of the communities in which they are located—in order to find support and nurture in the prophetic task.

But support does exist—whether it be in the form of groups who gather out of allegiance to a common cause, groups who gather regularly because of their ties of friendship, or small groups within communities who form bonds of trust and respect and become "safe places" for baring our souls. Such groups can not only provide would-be prophets support and encouragement; they also provide a place where we can honestly name our fears, talk about our successes and failures in prophetic witness, and (at best) be held accountable by those whose opinions we trust.

"The church," writes Bader-Saye "is that place where through baptism we have already faced death, our greatest fear, and seen it overcome. . . . If giving voice to fear is one way of keeping fear from controlling us, then the church needs to become a place where we are not embarrassed to hear the fears of others or to share our own."[23]

7. Reconnecting Our Unique Spiritual Gifts with Visionary, Prophetic Witness

Whatever we may say about the prophets of old, they were all *visionary leaders* who helped those around them envision the new reality that God wanted to create or was already at work creating in their midst. With Isaiah came the vision of God's making a way where there was no way in the wilderness (Isa. 35:6), of springs breaking forth in the desert (Isa. 35:8–10), and of a peaceable kingdom where wolf and lion and a little child would all play together (Isa. 11:1–9). With Micah came a vision of a world in which oppression of the poor would cease (Mic. 2) and in which God's people would instead "do justice, . . . love kindness, and . . . walk humbly with [their] God" (Mic. 6:8). And with Amos came a vision of a world in which justice rolled down like waters and righteousness like an ever-living stream (Amos 5:24).

I personally believe that what the church today most longs for are visionary leaders who speak to their people of an alternative future that can be believed and embraced and lived into. Like much of society around us, the church can easily fall prey to cynicism and despair. But the best antidote to such despair and cynicism is the alternative vision of God we glimpse in the gospel: a vision of a universe made new, whole, and fresh by a God who loves it inordinately and will not rest until that which is upside down is turned right side up—until the justice, righteousness, and *shalom* of God cover the earth as the waters cover the sea.

Such visionary leadership inevitably arises out of the unique giftedness of each individual and out of the Spirit's workings and stirrings within each life. Consequently, such leadership will be expressed differently by each one of us. Once again, my study of the Riverside preachers has been revelatory in this regard.

The Diverse Gifts of the Riverside Preachers

I was fascinated to discover during my research on the preaching at Riverside Church how very differently gifted each of Riverside's first five senior ministers were. Yet God used each one of them to bring prophetic visionary witness for a particular time and season in the life of church, nation, and world.[24]

Harry Emerson Fosdick, as I've already indicated, was really a pastor at heart, who spent three full afternoons a week in his study, meeting with people who came to him for counseling. A leader in the early pastoral care movement, he was fascinated with the intersection between psychology and pastoral care—in part because he himself had suffered an emotional breakdown during his seminary days and had spent a number of months recovering in a sanitarium. It was out of that experience that he also discovered the power of prayer, and his book *The Meaning of Prayer* became the all-time best seller of the fifty books he wrote during his ministry.

Because Fosdick cared passionately about individuals, he also cared about all the systems that affect a person's life—be they theological (as in the fundamentalist/modernist debate) or political (as in his stance on pacifism). And it was his love for individuals that led him to courageous prophetic witness.

Robert James "Jim" McCracken, who followed Fosdick, was a Baptist from Scotland who had a PhD in systematic theology and a career teaching theology in Scottish and Canadian universities before coming to Riverside. His sermons frequently reflected his theological bent, with titles like "What Is Meant by the Will of God?" or "In What Kind of God Do You Believe?" or "Where Protestants Differ from Roman Catholics and Why."

But McCracken also came to Riverside and to the United States as an immigrant, an outsider to our culture, and he brought with him an absolute bewilderment over the racism that was endemic in this land. During the 1950s—before, during, and after the 1954 *Brown vs. Board of Education* ruling by the U.S. Supreme Court—he repeatedly announced from the Riverside pulpit that "racism is a sin" and preached sermons like the one he gave in February 1954 titled "Discrimination, the Shame of Sunday Morning." By wedding his own life experience with his theology, he became a valued prophetic voice against racism at a critical time in our nation's history.

Ernest Campbell, Riverside's third senior pastor, had actually grown up a fundamentalist and had attended Bob Jones University before going to Princeton Theological Seminary. While at Princeton, he was introduced both to historical-critical biblical scholarship and to the study of Old Testament prophets and ended up doing his master's thesis there on the book of Amos.

Campbell's biblical grounding in the prophetic witness of the Scriptures fed his preaching at Riverside, enabling him to preach a number of visionary sermons. "The Case for Reparations" was based on the story of Zacchaeus, and he delivered it only a few weeks after James Forman interrupted worship at Riverside Church one May Sunday in 1969, demanding that the churches of the land make reparations to African Americans for long years of mistreatment. "An Open Letter to Billy Graham" was a 1972 sermon in which he castigated Graham for refusing to join with other religious leaders in urging President Nixon to stop the bombing of North Vietnam, telling him that "the President needs a Micaiah not a Zedekiah, a prophet, not a mere house chaplain."[25] And in 1974 Campbell preached "Overheard in Room 738," in which he invited the congregation into a hospital room to overhear three people with very different perspectives—two of them patients and one a hospital chaplain—discussing homosexuality. The latter sermon is remarkable for its time and ends with the chaplain opening the door toward the blessing of same-sex unions.

While Fosdick's prophetic witness began with a firm sense of God's love for individuals and then progressed outward to include national and global concerns, for William Sloane Coffin, Riverside's fourth senior pastor, the opposite was true:

> Because he believed God "so loved the world," Coffin also believed that the church should love the whole world. Consequently, his preaching challenged the church to move beyond nationalism, militarism, racism, sexism, heterosexism—whatever was blocking human ability to love the world—and to work for the kinds of structural changes that would make the world a more habitable place for all creatures.[26]

In a very real sense, that larger world—with all its political messiness and international intrigue—was Coffin's first home. Before going to seminary, Coffin, who was fluent in both Russian and French, had worked for the CIA in Germany, training Russians opposed to the Soviet government for operations inside the Soviet Union. While a chaplain at Yale University, he served as one of the initial advisers for the newly formed Peace Corps, took students to Guinea on an Operation Crossroads Africa Project, and was one of seven "Freedom Riders" who were arrested and convicted in Montgomery, Alabama, for protesting segregation. Coffin was also an outspoken critic of the Vietnam War who had been arrested in 1968, along with Dr. Benjamin Spock, for aiding and abetting draft resisters.

Coffin not only expressed his passionate and prophetic love for the world in his sermons at Riverside; he also wrote sermons that reflected on his equally prophetic deeds—such as blessing a shipment of wheat that was being sent to North Vietnam as an expression of reconciliation and peace after the war, or defying the U.S. government by going to Iran to lead a Christmas-day worship service for the American hostages held captive there.

Finally, Riverside's fifth pastor, James A. Forbes Jr., said that when he came to Riverside Church in 1989, he had three strikes going against him: he was Pentecostal (having been ordained a Pentecostal preacher and coming from a long line of Pentecostal preachers); he was a Southerner (having grown up in North Carolina during the civil rights struggles), and he was African American. But in his charismatic and prophetic ministry at Riverside, Forbes used all three of those life experiences to his advantage—preaching a gospel that consistently called on the American people to bring an end to racism and poverty, and doing so in a way that was consistent with his own African American Pentecostal style of witness and proclamation.

Sometimes I think we have a one-size-fits-all image of the prophetic mantle and believe that unless you are as fiery as William Sloane Coffin or as charismatic as James Forbes, you cannot be a prophet. But what impresses me about the witness of these preachers, when viewed as a whole, is how consistently they led from the very unique and particular strengths and gifts each had been given. When they offered those gifts to God and were willing to be used by God for visionary prophetic ministry in their own time and season, God also blessed and multiplied their efforts, calling others through them to join in prophetic witness as well.

The Resurrection Angel at Riverside Church

Perched high on the roof of The Riverside Church in New York is an angel blowing a trumpet and looking out toward the city. In one of my interviews with Dr. James Forbes, he spoke of that angel—known locally as the "resurrection angel"—as one who "knows what time it is and speaks a word that points the way we should go."[27]

I believe that the church today desperately needs preachers and lay witnesses who also "know what time it is" and who are willing to speak "a word [of God] that points the way we should go." We cannot become such visionary and prophetic witnesses in our own power, but in the power of God, ordinary men and women can become messengers of a prophetic gospel that God's whole beloved world longs to hear.

3

Speaking Truth in Love:
Strategies for Prophetic Proclamation

By its very nature, hate destroys and tears down;
by its very nature, love creates and builds up.
Love transforms with redemptive power.[1]
    Martin Luther King Jr., "Loving Your Enemies," in *Strength to Love*

When I graduated from seminary and went to serve in my first parish—a cluster of four small churches in central Virginia—I had a passion for prophetic preaching. The problem was, I didn't quite know how to go about it. My primary role models at the time were the biblical prophets, so I figured if I wasn't making people mad from time to time, I probably wasn't doing my job. But I also quickly learned that the prophets' style of confrontational, head-on witness didn't play very well in the parish. Indeed, if I had addressed my congregation as "you cows of Bashan" (Amos 4:1) or "you brood of vipers" (Matt. 3:7), I doubt they would have listened to me at all.

Pastors who live within the priestly and prophetic tensions of ministry know that one of the most difficult challenges in prophetic preaching is how to gain a hearing. How do we bring a difficult and often countercultural word from God to bear in such a way that people can actually hear and consider what we are saying?

The distinction Paul Tillich makes between "genuine" and "wrong" stumbling blocks in his book *Theology of Culture* is helpful in this regard.[2] Genuine stumbling blocks, says Tillich, are those theological affirmations that are at the heart of the gospel itself—those offenses that we dare not remove lest we rob preaching of its very heart and soul: offenses like a crucified messiah, a gospel that will lift up the lowly and send the rich empty away, or the radical call of Jesus to love and forgive our enemies. Helping people get beyond genuine stumbling blocks is not our work, says Tillich. It is God's work.

"Wrong" stumbling blocks, on the other hand, are those things we preachers may do—either intentionally or unintentionally in our communication of the gospel—that keep our congregations from giving the gospel we preach a fair hearing. They might include such things as arrogance or aloofness in the pulpit, the use of illustrations that belittle or put someone down, or failure to use inclusive language. False stumbling blocks are something we can and should do something about.

The challenge for prophetic preachers is how to get rid of the "wrong" stumbling blocks in our preaching without, at the same time, ridding our sermons of those "genuine" stumbling blocks that are at the heart of the biblical witness. For the goal is not to make our sermons more palatable; it is to make them more hearable.

This chapter explores ten strategies that prophetic preachers might use in making their sermons more accessible to listeners They are not all equally weighted. Indeed the first is clearly the most critical—the one that undergirds all the rest; without it, even the best of the other strategies may fail. Yet hopefully, when taken together, these strategies will give encouragement to preachers regarding what they are already doing well while also sparking the imagination toward new possibilities in prophetic witness.

SERMON DESIGN STRATEGIES

1. Speaking Truth *in Love*

Some years ago I invited a panel of laypeople to come into a class I was teaching and talk to us about preaching from their vantage point of sitting in the pew each Sunday. "What are you hoping you will receive in the sermon when you go to church on Sunday morning?" I asked them.

At one juncture in the conversation, one of the laypeople on that panel—a man who managed a doctor's office—said something like this: "I know that one of the things I hope my pastor will give me is a different perspective on the world and on life than the one I usually hear around me. Frankly, I hope she will confront me from time to time and challenge me regarding some of the justice issues facing us as a community and nation."

He went on to tell us that his pastor was well known in his community for her outspokenness on justice and peace issues. "Jean and I do not always see eye to eye on things," he continued, "but I trust her. I know that when she brings difficult words to us, she does so because she loves us and she genuinely wants us to grow in Christ. She also practices what she preaches."

Ernest Freemont Tittle

In his book *Speaking Truth in Love*, Philip Wogaman tells about Ernest Freemont Tittle, one of the great prophetic preachers of the mid-twentieth century who held a number of fairly radical views that were not broadly shared by his congregation at First Methodist Church in Evanston, Illinois. At one juncture in Tittle's ministry a serious move was mounted by some members of the congregation to have him removed from the pulpit. But the tide, Wogaman says, was stemmed when a leading layman in the congregation—widely known for his conservatism—put a stop to the idea with a moving speech about how Dr. Tittle had stayed up all night with the layman's dying wife.[3]

Wogaman writes,

> Let me state the principle in an academic way. A C-plus sermon will be perceived as a B-plus or A-minus if the preacher is viewed as a friend; an A-plus sermon will be demoted to a B or lower if the preacher comes across as uncaring.
>
> But this is not finally an academic principle, not finally even a question of effectiveness. It has the closest possible relationship to the content, not just the form, of preaching. If the whole point of the prophetic word is God's love, how on earth can that message be heard if it is not expressed in a context of love? . . . We cannot preach about love unlovingly; it is a self-contradiction.[4]

If prophetic preaching is born out of thinly disguised anger at a congregation, out of frustration with a congregation, or out of a desire to appear loving so that the message will be heard and accepted, people will know it. We cannot fake love in the pulpit.

On the other hand, if the message we bring is genuinely born out of love—a love regularly practiced for even the most recalcitrant of sinners—hearts may well be opened to the prophetic message of the gospel in ways we cannot even begin to imagine or anticipate. As Wogaman rightly notes, this is at heart not a practical matter but a theological one, issuing from the way that God in Christ deals with us.

2. Starting with the Familiar and Moving toward the Unfamiliar

One strategy Barbara Lundblad suggests to help people move through resistance to change in preaching is to begin with that which is more familiar and comfortable for the hearers, and then move toward that which is less familiar and more stretching for them.[5] Such an approach allows the hearers to ease into a new idea without immediately becoming defensive and resistant to it.

Tex Sample's Sermon on Peace

Tex Sample, a sociologist of religion who has long encouraged us preachers to attend more closely to the needs of blue-collar and "hard-living" folk in our proclamation, tells of an experience he had as a guest preacher in a church in the Southwest in which he used this strategy effectively.[6] When the pastor first invited him to preach, he told Sample that he wanted him to preach a sermon on peace and to simply "lay it out" straight and preach from his heart. But when Sample arrived on the scene, the pastor informed him that the congregation was actually very much a "hawkish" church in which half the members were also members of the military, with the other half being blue-collar and lower-to-middle-class sales and service folk who tended to be very conservative in their thinking. At 9 p.m. on Saturday night, the pastor told Sample that he might want to keep these things in mind when he preached the next morning.

Sample reports that he went back to his hotel room and immediately began rewriting his sermon so that people in that context might be able to hear what he had to say. He decided to start his sermon by telling the congregation about his own cross-country flight to get to the church. He told them he had one of those clear, picture-perfect days for flying in which there were no clouds to block his view, so he had four to five hours to see the beautiful and varied landscapes of America from sea to shining sea. He also told them how much he loved his country and wanted peace for its land.

Sample moved on from that opening story to talk about other people in other lands who also loved their countries and longed for peace,

and how important it was—if peace was going to come to our world—
for there to be an end to the upbuilding and stockpiling of nuclear
weapons. "Surely many people there disagreed with some, maybe most,
of what I said," Sample writes, "but they listened. . . . I made contact
with *their* approach to meaning, with *their* love of country, and in that
context, they trusted me enough to let me say things they otherwise
would not have tolerated gladly."[7]

James Forbes's Sermon at Riverside Church

James Forbes, the retired pastor of Riverside Church in New York City,
does a similar thing in a sermon he preached there. Listen to the pro-
gression he makes as he moves from the more familiar to the less familiar with his own congregation:

> Years ago, when I was still living in North Carolina, someone said to
> me, "Brother Forbes, do you think the gospel can be preached by
> someone who is not Pentecostal?" Well, I wasn't sure, for it was the
> only preaching I had known, but I imagined that it could happen
> even if I hadn't seen or heard it. Indeed, I found out some time later
> that it was so.
>
> After I had moved away from my hometown, someone said to me,
> "Reverend Forbes, have you ever heard the true gospel from a white
> preacher?" Well, in theory I knew it had to be true, for God doesn't
> withhold the Spirit from anyone. Though I had my doubts that a
> white preacher could speak with power, I came to a point in my life
> where I had to say, "Yes, I've heard it!"
>
> Some time went by, and people began to press upon me the
> question of the ordination of women. "Could the gospel be preached
> by a woman even though the holy scriptures bid a woman to keep
> silence in the church?" I had to ponder this, for it went against what
> I had known in my own church and there was much resistance from
> my brother clergy. But I listened to my sisters and before too long I
> knew the Spirit of God was calling them to preach. Who was I to get
> in God's way?
>
> Now I thought I had been asked the last question about who
> might be called to bring me the word of the Lord. But I found out I
> was wrong. A new question has been posed to me and many of you
> know what it is. "Can gay men and lesbian women be called to preach
> the word of God?" Oh, I know what the Bible says and I know what

my own uneasiness says and I can see that same uneasiness in some
of your faces. But I've been wrong before, and the Spirit has been
nudging me to get over my uneasiness. Sometimes we forget Jesus'
promise—that the Spirit will lead us into all truth. Well, that must
have meant the disciples didn't know it all then, and maybe we don't
know it all now.[8]

By starting with the familiar and comfortable and then pressing toward
the unfamiliar and the uncomfortable, we can allow people the time
and the space to have their horizons stretched from the inside out. And
in the process, we can also establish points of identification with them
that strengthen the bonds between pastor and people—even while prophetic words are being spoken.

3. Standing in the Shoes of Another and Viewing the World from a Different Perspective

Several years ago Holly Haile Davis, an ordained Presbyterian pastor who
is also a Shinnecock Indian, preached a sermon for a meeting of Long
Island Presbytery titled "Three Moons in My Moccasins."[9] She invited
her hearers to see the world from the vantage point of her own Shinnecock tribe, where the median family income on the reservation was (in
2000) $14,000 a year, where families struggled to hold on to their small
homes in the face of rampant real estate development, and where city
and state "have joined the howling pack of those who challenge the Shinnecock Nation's right to exist."[10] She challenged her hearers to become
active seekers of justice on behalf of oppressed peoples, and she closed
her sermon with this prayer: "Great Spirit, grant that I may not judge my
siblings until I have walked for three moons in their moccasins."[11]

One of the strategies preachers can employ when seeking to open
new worlds of understanding for their hearers is to invite them to "walk
three moons" in someone else's shoes. For often, when we step out
of our own comfort zones and enter the world of another, we see the
world—and God's purposes for us within it—differently.

Barbara K. Lundblad, "An Easy Chair at the Laundromat"[12]

Lutheran pastor and professor Barbara Lundblad begins one of her
sermons—based on the story of the rich man and Lazarus in Luke's

Gospel (Luke 16:19–31) and preached to an ecumenical group of pastors—by telling about a pastor friend who while ministering to a poor community in Detroit asked a group of mothers one day what they would do if they won the lottery.

> "What would I do if I won the lottery?" one woman said. "I'd buy easy chairs for the Laundromat—enough chairs so everybody could sit down and take a load off. All they've got is three old chairs, and two have broken seats—and the one that's not broken is so hard you'd rather sit on a dryer and burn your—you know what I mean, Pastor."[13]

The pastor went on to press the point, asking the woman if there weren't anything else she'd want to do with the money, but she held firm. No, she said. Just chairs for the laundromat.

Lundblad uses this story to open up—in a very personal way— the reality of the gap between the rich and the poor in this land, and the fact that while some in our country are purchasing expensive watches at Cartier, many of the poor desire only to have basic needs met, for themselves or for others that they care for. She ultimately uses her sermon to encourage preachers to challenge the language often heard in the public arena that portrays the poor as lazy, lacking in motivation, having too many illegitimate children, and cheating the government, and that urges the adoption of policies that will only further widen the chasm. She concludes her sermon by saying,

> Those of us who claim to speak in Christ's name are called to share his vision. . . . If we speak in the name of Jesus we must see Lazarus and love him, love him back to life again. We hardly know where to begin to close the chasm between the rich and the poor on this side of heaven. We could begin by talking to the women in the Laundromat, and by listening—really listening—to the One who has risen from the dead.[14]

Emilie Townes, "The Valley before the Vision"

In a sermon she preached for a "Coming Out Day" worship service at Yale Divinity School, womanist theologian Emilie Townes also invited her hearers to stand in the shoes of another. Only in this instance, she was asking her hearers to stand more fully in the shoes of the gay, lesbian, bisexual, and transgendered (GLBT) persons who were already in their midst.

Townes's text for the day was Ezekiel 37, in which the prophet is taken to the valley of dry bones and told to prophesy to them. Ezekiel, she contended, was a counter voice to the "don't worry, be happy" theology that many false prophets of the time were espousing. Rather than offering a quick and easy fix for the people's pain, Ezekiel, the "least sympathetic of all the prophets," first told the people that their suffering would indeed be very long. He acknowledged the depths of their pain and suffering before he held out for them a vision of hope.

you see, ezekiel realized that you can't rush healing
    and you can't make things all right
    until the person is ready for it

but we often move too hastily to console the wounded
    assuring them that everything will be all right
in our rush to help
    we cover up their pain
                diffuse their agony
                and ignore their misery
before *they've* had a chance to even experience the pain for themselves

we don't want to accept
    their tears or anger or questioning
    because it means that we might have to cry with them
        or admit our anger
        or face the questions *we* have for our lives

ezekiel's dream recognized the need for the valley before the vision.[15]

Townes went on to name in very specific ways the pain that GLBT persons suffer, while inviting the community to stand with them in their suffering. She also invited those who were suffering to acknowledge and address the pain, before embracing God's promise to them in the midst of it. She concluded her sermon with these words:

can you hear these bones of mine rattling
    with the promise of salvation
come on winds of deliverance
God's grace is getting good to me now
whoooooweeeee pain, God's grace
    there in the laughter
    there through the tears
    there in the agony

there in the ecstasy
there in the morning
there in the night
there in the fear
there in the boldness
there in the earth, wind, rain and fire
ummph . . . ummph . . . ummph . . . have mercy pain, i've got to go

4. Standing *With* the Congregation Rather than *Opposite* the Congregation

Walter Brueggemann draws what has proved for me a very helpful and insightful analogy between preaching and family systems theory. He says that in most church situations of biblical interpretation three voices are operative: that of the biblical text, that of the pastor, and that of the congregation. Yet all too often pastors team up with texts to "triangle" against their congregations in preaching, leaving the congregation "a hostile, resistant outsider." How much better, contends Brueggemann, if the pastor stands with the congregation against the text, letting the radical Word of God offend both![16]

In a sermon he preached on the "blessings" and "woes" in Luke's version of the Beatitudes, Baptist pastor and professor David Bartlett tells about his own experience in shifting in sermon preparation from standing against the congregation to standing with them under God's prophetic Word.

> Some years ago when I was a pastor near the University of Chicago, the lectionary handed me a text from Amos, as tough as the text from Jeremiah we just heard. I wrote a pointed sermon reminding the members of my congregation that they lived in middle class and upper middle class wealth in a tiny little section of the city surrounded on three sides by poverty and on the fourth side by Lake Michigan.
>
> It was a stunning sermon. And as I sat at the typewriter (this was a long time ago), my adrenaline surged with righteous indignation.
>
> Then I made a risky move. I showed the sermon to my wife, Carol Bartlett. "And where do you live?" she said. "And how many Rockefellers exploited how many workers to build your splendid Baptist pension fund?" I shifted the sermon. Instead of speaking for the prophet, I tried to listen to the prophet.[17]

Brian Blount, "Stay Close"[18]

While I was on the faculty of Princeton Theological Seminary I heard New Testament scholar Brian Blount also make a decision to "stand with" his hearers in a sermon he preached to graduating seniors. The sermon, titled "Stay Close," was based on the story in Mark 9:14–29 where Jesus heals a demon-possessed boy and then challenges the disciples to pray harder so that they, too, can cast out demons in his name. In his sermon, Blount issued a strong challenge to seminarians to stay close to God through prayer so that they, too, might be empowered by God to cast out the many demons of injustice they would face in their ministries.

Toward the sermon's end, we find these very honest and self-revealing words, spoken by the preacher. Listen to how Blount, by his own honest identification with the fears of these budding pastors, also enhances the power and authenticity of his proclamation:

> But before I close I must come clean myself. You know, when I first heard about this invitation [to preach to you graduates], my first inclination was to turn it down. Not because I'm not honored that you would ask me to preach at such an important occasion (which I am), but because I was a little afraid. Not of preaching, but of preaching in this academic context. I never preached in this chapel while I was a student, and when I returned, I honestly intended not to preach here as a professor. When I was a student it was because it always felt more like an academic exercise than a spiritual one because I felt, even then, that I was being graded. Now it's because I remember how my sermons in my community in Virginia sometimes got me into trouble, and junior professors already have all the trouble they can handle just by being junior professors. I worry about that kind of stuff all the time, it seems now. About how people perceive me. About whether I'm doing too much. Saying too much. About how far I have the resources to push myself beyond the confines of this sheltered seminary existence to work where I ought to be working in the world around it. . . .
>
> Believe me, there will come a time when you start to worry in the same way. Worry about offending parishioners, threatening the budget, offending powerful people on the session, in the presbytery, on the deacons' board, in the bishop's office, in the mayor's office, on the school board, on the chamber of commerce, in the PTS community, and you start to think, you know, "I've got a family. I want to have

friends. I want people to like me. I want to keep my job or secure it for a long time." So you start to think, "Maybe I ought to do Christianity, do faith the way Brian Blount plays basketball, without risk, without doing anything that might push me to the point of no return." I'm here tonight, though, because I want to tell you, and remind myself, if that's what you've graduated to do, then maybe your presbytery can use you, maybe your bishop can use you, maybe your church can use you.

But I'm not so sure God can use you.

'Appears to me, by then you're pretty much all used up. God needs soldiers, not used-up followers. God needs players who can give God twenty points every night. That's what finally came to me as I meditated on the decision to worship with you this evening. I thought about my father struggling and believing, I thought about those slaves singing and believing. In cotton fields, in cornfields, in tobacco fields, in fields of misery and hopelessness, and yet they sang the Lord's song in a foreign land. They stayed close to God, and that gave them faith and the faith gave them power.[19]

By taking his stand *with* the congregation under the Word of God, and by openly acknowledging the ways in which that Word also convicts him, Blount is able to speak some challenging words in a very hearable way.

5. Using a Congregation's History as a Bridge to a Prophetic Vision for Its Future

One of the realities of congregations is that people are often far more likely to embrace a new vision for the future if they see it as being in continuity with valued traditions of the past than if it seems to come to them "out of the blue" without any connection to who they are or have been as a people of God. Consequently, wise pastors will learn to use the congregation's own history as a bridge in articulating prophetic visions for the future.

Timothy Hart-Andersen, "The Prophetic Voice of the Church"[20]

As part of the 150th anniversary celebration of Westminster Presbyterian Church in Minneapolis, Minnesota, pastor Timothy Hart-

Andersen preached a sermon titled "The Prophetic Voice of the Church" in which he encouraged the congregation toward prophetic witness in the future by reminding them of their prophetic witness in the past. He focused on the decade of the 1970s—a tumultuous time in our nation's history during which, he reminded them, "Watergate happened. President Nixon resigned. Jimmy Carter and Walter Mondale were elected, but the Iranian crisis doomed a second term."[21]

He also recounted some of the prophetic initiatives of the church during that decade. The church established its first Task Force on Religion and Race, and it initiated a Town Hall Forum, with Watergate prosecutor Archibald Cox as the first speaker. The church welcomed to its staff a Chinese pastor in order to continue the ministry to Chinese immigrants the congregation had begun in the late nineteenth century. The church's pastor at the time preached a sermon denouncing President Nixon's decision to bomb Hanoi on Christmas Eve 1972. And during that decade the church also ordained its first women elders and called its first woman as minister.

Hart-Andersen did not try to pretend that the church had been a completely faithful prophetic witness throughout its history. Indeed he was honest about places at which the church was slow to act or had failed to act. But by naming the congregation's past faithfulness, he also encouraged them—on the occasion of their 150th anniversary—to consider prophetic witness as a significant part of their future calling as a people of God.

William Sloane Coffin, "Warring Madness"[22]

One of the most famous sermons William Sloane Coffin preached while he was pastor of The Riverside Church was titled "Warring Madness." Coffin preached the sermon only six months into his pastorate there and used it to announce a major new initiative on nuclear disarmament that would be based out of Riverside Church and headed by community organizer Cora Weiss. However, Coffin also wisely framed his sermon in terms of Riverside's past history.

First, he chose to preach "Warring Madness" on May 21, 1978, the Sunday closest to the 100th anniversary of the birth of Harry Emerson Fosdick, Riverside's much-beloved founding pastor.

Second, Coffin quoted two of Fosdick's most famous sermons—beginning with "Shall the Fundamentalists Win?" and then moving toward the sermon in which Fosdick declared his own commitment to pacifism, "The Unknown Soldier" (preached on Armistice Day, 1933). By so doing Coffin reminded the congregation that the church had been since its founding involved in peacemaking efforts, and he helped them see their new initiative as being in continuity with their past.

Finally, Coffin announced that the disarmament project would be established in Fosdick's honor and encouraged members of the church to give generously in his name "to change the arms race into a peace race." He concluded his sermon with these words:

> We, too, must carry on a lover's quarrel with the world, so that when, like Harry Emerson Fosdick, we depart this life, we leave behind a little more truth, a little more justice, a little more peace, a little more beauty than would have been there had we not cared enough about the human race to quarrel with it, not for what it is, but for what it might be.[23]

6. Using a Congregation's Current Mission Involvement as a Bridge for Prophetic Witness

Preachers can build bridges in sermons not only between congregational history and prophetic witness; they can also build bridges between current congregational mission and prophetic witness. In almost every congregation I know, the people of God are already involved in some kind of ministry to alleviate pain and suffering in their community and in the larger world. The wise pastor will work to forge links between this mission engagement and the larger social and systemic evils that are addressed from the pulpit.

For example, if the church is involved in a ministry that brings congregants into contact with recent immigrants to the United States, the pastor might begin with some of the stories that have arisen out of those contacts in order to frame a sermon that deals with the larger systemic issue of immigration reform. If the church is involved in ministries that help feed the hungry in the community, the pastor might draw on that involvement in a sermon that addresses the current economic crisis in our nation and how it is affecting those who are struggling most to survive. Or if the youth group has been involved in a mission work trip to some part of the nation or world where poverty is pervasive, the pastor might use that involvement as a link to address global poverty and its systemic causes.

There are several good reasons for forging such links in prophetic sermons. First, by linking local mission and prophetic witness, one affirms congregations for the good deeds they are already doing and encourages them to build on their best instincts (rather than castigating them for not doing all they might). Second, people can often entertain global and systemic issues more readily if they are first incarnated in a local, personal way. And finally, people need to have links made between charity and good works, on the one hand, and activism in the public arena, on the other. If they can come to view activism as an extension of charity, it may help break down some of the resistances congregations often have in moving from one to the other.

James A. Forbes Jr., "Emancipation from Poverty"[24]

Dr. James A. Forbes Jr. illustrates the building of a bridge between the church's current benevolent mission and larger systemic causes of poverty in a sermon at Riverside Church in New York City on the weekend celebrating the birthday of Martin Luther King Jr. The sermon, titled "Emancipation from Poverty" and based on Jesus' sermon in Luke 4, presses the church to embrace not only King's call to racial equality but also his call for an elimination of poverty. Forbes recounts that Carlyle Marney, a progressive Baptist preacher from North Carolina, had once said to him, "Jim, you're going to discover that when we get through working on the race issue, that's just intramural sports in comparison to the class issue." Forbes then comments, "How right he was!"[25] He goes on to acknowledge the many benevolent works in which Riverside Church was involved while also pressing them to go further in realizing King's and Jesus' dreams:

> The Riverside Church has always been involved in benevolent works. We give grants to community groups that empower disadvantaged people. We take up offerings at Christmas and Easter. At a level that most people are not aware of, in our regular church programming we're involved in attempts to bridge the poverty gaps in people's lives. The Black Christian Caucus attempts to provide scholarships to enable our students to prepare for the new agenda of a society where race and class will no longer hamper the capacity for people to fulfill their destinies. Our prison ministry awards grants to inmates and former inmates and families of inmates, and our children prepare gifts for mothers who are inmates to offer something to their

children. Our social-service ministry is extensive. We have a food pantry. We have a homeless shelter. . . . We have a clothing drive. . . . We have small emergency grants. . . . We have decided as a council to invest a portion of our endowment and portfolio in South Africa and in neighborhood minority enterprises. . . . The list could go on and on.

We have been involved. But I find myself wondering: is it time to hear Jesus all over again? "Today this scripture has been fulfilled in your hearing." Is there a Christian congregation that is prepared to hear Dr. King with respect to class action, to hear that simply helping one or two poor people here and there will not be enough? To hear that helping our own neighborhood is not enough? To hear that there is a *system of impoverishment* and that that system is structurally designed so that all our little benevolent works will not really change anything long term until the systems themselves are changed? Our good deeds may bring momentary amelioration to a few, but until the system has been confronted, the system that perpetuates the evil notion that poverty is acceptable, the kingdom of God cannot and will not be advanced.[26]

By listing all the ways the congregation is already involved in trying to eliminate poverty, Forbes both affirms and acknowledges their commitment to the cause. However, he also stretches them further—urging them to embrace the fullness of King's dream and to become not only advocates for individuals but also agents for social and structural change.

7. Inviting Someone Personally Involved in the Concern to Participate in Preaching on It

It is one thing to invite congregants imaginatively to enter the world of another. It is another thing altogether to invite someone who is actually involved in the concern at hand to talk from a first-person perspective about the issue and how it affects his or her life.

Susan Murtha and Sharon Cody, "Finding the Right Well"[27]

Several years ago I attended the First Congregational Church in Guilford, Connecticut, when the associate pastor, Susan Murtha, preached on the woman at the well in John's Gospel. Before she began her sermon she told us that she had invited Sharon Cody, a former inmate at York Correctional Institution, to participate with her in the sermon, sharing her own experience in a transitional program for women released from prison. The transitional program for prisoners was also a new mission initiative for the church.

Murtha began her sermon, titled "Finding the Right Well," by offering some reflections on the text for the day from John 4:1–42. She set the scene for Jesus' encounter with the woman at the well, marveled at the range of conversation the two of them had, and concluded her introduction with these words:

> The conversation begins when Jesus asks for a drink of water from a woman caught in an endless cycle of drawing water at the well. Today we talk personally with someone who knows what it means to be caught in endless cycles and is willing to share with us her experience of finding the right well to quench the thirst.

Murtha then invited Sharon Cody to come forward and join her in the chancel area. As they sat there together in two comfortable chairs, Murtha interviewed Cody about her life experiences. She began by asking Cody to tell about her own difficulties in staying out of prison and the reasons it had been hard for her. She then asked about her experience with the transitional program and why this time had been different for her. Finally, she asked her to share something of her experience of grace and faith in the midst of it all. (Since Cody had previously told her story to the church's prison ministry committee, Murtha knew which questions to ask.)

The congregation was deeply moved by Cody's testimony in church that day—a testimony filled with struggle and faith, gratitude and joy in her new postprison life. (Cody now works for the women prisoners' transitional program.) By bracketing her testimony within the story of the woman at the well, Murtha also gave the hearers a framework for hearing it—and the biblical story—in a new way.

After Cody told her story, Murtha invited the congregation to respond with "Amen." She then returned to the pulpit and shared some concluding reflections about the ways that Jesus offers living water to all who thirst. She praised the woman at the well for being the first evangelist in John's Gospel—a witness who, like Sharon Cody, moved people with her testimony.

William Sloane Coffin, "AIDS"[28]

A second example comes from a sermon William Sloane Coffin preached at the height of the AIDS epidemic in New York City. At a time when some churches in the city were refusing even to provide funerals for people who had died of AIDS and when misinformation about the disease abounded, Coffin preached a sermon simply titled "AIDS." He began the sermon by contrasting the deaths of those who die surrounded by flowers, music, family, and friends with the deaths of those who die largely abandoned because they died of AIDS. He then debunked some of the myths surrounding the disease: that AIDS is only a disease of gay men, that it is only a disease of the promiscuous, and that it can be spread by air. He called the church and city to task for their roles in abandoning people with AIDS while also giving testimony to the grace he had received from individuals within the Riverside congregation who were battling AIDS.

Coffin concluded his sermon by asking Jim Johnson, a member of the congregation who been diagnosed with AIDs, to give his own testimony of faith. Johnson told of his experience with the disease—of how he had lost his job, didn't feel well much of the time, and was now on disability. He also gave testimony to the faithfulness of his lover, Tom, in caring for him, and to the care and support he had found at Riverside Church. He then offered this challenge to the church:

> To be a Christian is to be in community, and more so here at Riverside than elsewhere. Those of us who have AIDS can be open to what this community offers us. And for those who are not ill there is an opportunity to reach out to the ill and to make their final days more comfortable, to help bring about spiritual acceptance with respect to death, to make this church a haven of love and support in Jesus Christ.[29]

He concluded his testimony (and the sermon) by reciting the 23rd Psalm, which he termed "one of the great comforting psalms of my faith."[30]

My guess is that for many in the congregation, AIDS took on a human face that day, when one of their own dared to speak openly about his battle with it. What wisdom Coffin exhibited as a preacher both in inviting Jim Johnson to participate with him in the proclamation that morning—and in allowing him to have the final word.

8. Articulating the Opposing Viewpoint in a Manner That Is Fair and Accurate

During the time that I was on the faculty of Princeton Theological Seminary, a number of faculty members contributed to a book of essays in which they articulated various theological and biblical positions on the issue of homosexuality. One evening the seminary hosted an open forum where students and faculty entered into debate, and Nancy Duff, a Christian ethicist, was the moderator. At the outset Duff laid down several helpful ground rules for our discussion. But the one I most remember is this: "If you are going to respond to the point of view of someone who differs with you in this discussion, you need to be able to state your opponent's position so clearly and so fairly that your opponent could say, 'Yes, that is what I mean.' Only then are you free to argue your own position."[31]

Her ground rule is not only good guidance for fair debate; it is also good guidance for fair preaching. If we are going to tackle the position of someone who disagrees with us in a sermon, it is important that we state that person's position as fairly and as accurately as we can. Otherwise, we can easily raise the ire and the defenses of people who feel that we've diminished or misrepresented their points of view in our preaching.

William Sloane Coffin's Preparation for Preaching

In his book *Preaching Christian Doctrine*, William J. Carl shares these insights about how Bill Coffin prepared for preaching:

> Coffin does not avoid the "emotionally explosive"; he ignites it. But he never does so foolishly or dogmatically. The reason is that he knows what he is talking about. Not everyone will agree with Coffin's conclusions on issues, but no one questions his knowledge of the problem.
>
> Coffin always does his homework. He sets aside time and reads articles and books—whatever he can get his hands on. He reads both sides of an issue. When he emerges from his study, he knows the history of the problem, the political and social dimensions, and the various arguments and questions for the modern Christian to ponder. . . .
>
> He does not attempt a major moral problem every week. In fact, his practice has been to immerse himself in one major problem for a

period of time. In the early sixties it was civil rights. In the late sixties to early seventies it was Vietnam. In the late seventies it was hunger and American intervention in places like El Salvador. In the eighties it has been the arms race. . . . At Yale and at Riverside his practice has been to do his homework and make his statement clearly and early to the congregation only once, and not badger them with it week after week. Most of the time he preaches the lectionary and deals with pastoral issues.[32]

My own study of Coffin's sermons reinforces the truth of Carl's statements. Though some of Coffin's critics at Riverside Church accused him of only preaching on one theme during the 1980s and early nineties—namely, nuclear disarmament—his sermons do not bear that out. They are varied and often highly pastoral and, as Carl notes, ordinarily lectionary based. I also find it interesting that Coffin's most famous sermon, "Alex's Death," preached only two weeks after his own twenty-four-year-old son was tragically killed in an automobile accident, deals with that most personally existential of all issues: death.

However, when Coffin does preach on a social issue, it is clear that he has done his homework and done it well. The result is that he is able to articulate the opposing point of view clearly and accurately. Even if you disagree with him, you know he has at least entertained and considered other points of view along the way. And if you want to argue with him, you had best be equally prepared!

9. The Court Jester: Lampooning the Principalities and Powers

Charles Campbell, professor of homiletics at Duke Divinity School, argues that when we are preaching prophetically, we are also going up against principalities and powers that oppose God's ways. Therefore, we need to look for ways to disarm and silence them through nonviolent resistance. One way he suggests we do so is by lampooning them—sort of a *Saturday Night Live* approach to preaching.

Campbell notes that in Walter Wink's interpretation of Matthew 5:40, where Jesus tells his hearers that if someone takes their cloak, they should "give [their] inner one also," he sees Jesus to be engaging in such lampooning himself.

The situation is one in which the economic powers have so milked the poor that all they have left to be sued for are their garments.

When their outer garment is claimed in court, Wink argues, Jesus counsels them to give the inner one also. That is, the victim of the economic system, who has no other recourse, takes off the inner garment and walks out of court stark naked. In this way the victim not only retains his or her status as a moral agent, but also unmasks the system's essential cruelty and "burlesques its pretensions to justice, law and order." As the person walks out of court naked and people on the streets begin to ask what is going on, the economic system itself stands naked and is exposed for what it is—a system that treats the poor as "sponges[s] to be squeezed dry by the rich."[33]

Campbell suggests that using a comic and burlesque style in preaching can be a powerful way to name and expose the powers:

> Rather than somber, self-important sermons dealing with such matters as capitalism or individualism, preachers from time to time may offer startlingly comic or burlesque depictions of the powers, lampooning the absurdity of their claims. Then a space may be created for the redemptive power of the Word, not just for the hearers, but for the powers themselves.[34]

I cannot read Campbell's words without recalling one of the speeches Archbishop Desmond Tutu made during the height of the antiapartheid movement in South Africa. In it he addressed the minister of law and order of South Africa with these words: "Mr. Minister, we must remind you that you are not God. You are just a man. And one day your name shall merely be a faint scribble on the pages of history, while the name of Jesus Christ, the Lord of the church, shall live forever. . . ."[35] Through his own lampooning, Tutu reminds us of who the true Sovereign of the world is—and by contrast, he shows us that the pretend emperor has no clothes.

10. Taking the Long View

Finally, I want to talk about taking the long view in prophetic preaching—for I think it is important that pastors do so in order to avoid becoming discouraged.

In my early years of ministry I tended to think that change in people's lives and in the life of a congregation happened either immediately or not at all. So if I preached a few prophetic sermons and nothing much happened, I considered my people to be recalcitrant and myself to be a faithful, if ineffective, change agent.

Over time, though, I have come to realize that for most of us change happens slowly and imperceptibly over the space of years. Genuine transformation in preaching often follows a similar trajectory. Barbara Lundblad puts it well when she says, "Transformational preaching takes place over time. There may be a rare life-changing sermon, but more often it is a lifetime of sermons inviting the listener into God's alternative vision that leads to transformation."[36]

I once heard someone say of the pastor of his congregation that one of the things he most admired about him was his patience with his flock and the way his overall preaching reflected a long-term strategy for transformation rather than an episodic or immediate one.

"Here's the pattern I've observed," he said. "For three weeks out of the month, my pastor will preach sermons the congregation has pretty much come to expect from him: sermons that are full of grace and love and encouragement and pastoral care. But about every fourth week, there will be this sermon with a zinger in the middle of it that really stretches our edges and challenges us in some area. And because they come as a part of the whole package, our people are usually very open to hearing them.

"I've seen this happen so many times over the years," he continued, "that I have to believe this strategy is intentional on our pastor's part. He knows we need to hear those stretching sermons that challenge us to take the next step in our journey of faith. But he also knows we'll hear them better if they are enshrouded in the midst of sermons that offer us lots of love and grace."

One of the phenomena I have observed through the years is that, for whatever reason, people tend to hear prophetic sermons louder than others. You can preach ten predominantly pastoral sermons and one prophetic sermon, and the one that will be heard the loudest is the prophetic one. Frankly, I think we need to acknowledge this reality and plan our preaching accordingly. The balance of our preaching is not measured by how many sermons we preach on this or that issue but by how people hear us. And in prophetic ministry, as well as in all forms of ministry, there is good biblical and theological rationale for erring on the side of grace. After all, that is what God in Christ has consistently done with us.

CONCLUSION

Some years ago I had a conversation with the pastor of a small congregation in New Jersey about her seminary intern. The intern (someone I also knew) fled her native country some years ago as a political refugee and has a strong social consciousness. "How is it going with her preaching?" I asked. Susan (the pastor) laughed and said that basically it was going well. "It's taken some adjustment," she said, "because, as you know, this intern has a very strong prophetic edge to her preaching and really isn't afraid to tackle anything from the pulpit. In fact, around here we refer to her as our 'cheeky preacher.'"

"But you know," she continued, "our congregation has really grown to love her, and she, us. And the great thing about this internship is that she is not only stretching and challenging our congregation with her prophetic witness from the pulpit; they are also challenging her to think not only about *what* she wants to say in the pulpit, but *how best to get it heard.*"

Frankly, that's a pretty good summary of what I think the church today needs more of: cheeky preachers who also know how to get their message heard.

4

Giving Shape to the Witness: Forms for Prophetic Preaching

> Instead of thinking of sermon form and content as separate realities, it is far more accurate to speak of the form of the content. A sermon's form, though often largely unperceived by the hearers, provides shape and energy to the sermon and thus becomes itself a vital force in how a sermon makes meaning.[1]
>
> Thomas G. Long, *The Witness of Preaching*, 2nd ed.

When a pastor sets out to prepare a sermon that involves prophetic witness, the forms for doing so are as broad as the preacher's own imagination. Indeed, one of the delights of preaching is the opportunity it affords for experimentation with form. As in all artistic endeavors, form follows function in sermon preparation. Until the preacher knows what she wants to say, she cannot determine how best to say it. But once she knows what she wants her sermon to say and to do,[2] she is ready to give it shape.

In this chapter I discuss a variety of forms that prophetic preaching can take. In each instance I also illustrate the form by providing an example of a prophetic sermon that has been preached using it. Some are classic forms that have stood the test of time; others are newer and more experimental forms. But all of them can be effective if used in the right place at the right time with the right message.

A DOZEN PROPHETIC SERMON FORMS

1. Invitation to Dialogue

One way to preach prophetic sermons more pastorally is to use them as an invitation to dialogue around a particular topic or concern. The preacher's word, in this instance, is not the "last word" on a topic but a word that initiates ongoing conversation within the congregation. Such preaching, while taking a stand, is also respectful of those who disagree with the preacher's point of view. Depending on the congregation and its patterns, the actual dialogue might take place within the worship service, after the service (perhaps in a "sermon talk-back" session with the pastor), via e-mails or follow-up conversations with parishioners, or over a series of weeks in adult education classes. What is important is that an opportunity for response is given.

In the sermon below, Scott Black Johnston makes the case for same-sex marriage on biblical, theological, and biological grounds. He states his own beliefs clearly and succinctly while also leaving room for people in the congregation to disagree with him. Indeed, he uses the sermon as an invitation to dialogue about the issue at hand.

Scott Black Johnston, "Blessing and Cursing"[3] (James 3:1–10)

Introduction. Black Johnston tells his congregation that he has been involved in videotaping a series for a new program on the Hallmark Channel that will begin airing the following fall. The series will feature a group of diverse clergy, gathered for breakfast at a local greasy spoon, debating various topics. The second topic in the series was to be focused on the question "Should marriage be only between a man and a woman?" Since Black Johnston didn't want his congregation first learning his viewpoints via a 45-second television sound bite, he designed a sermon series on "God and Human Relationships." In the intervening time, the producers of the series decided not to air the gay-marriage show, but Black Johnston was already committed to preach on the topic.

The Invitation

William Sloane Coffin, chaplain of Yale University and later pastor of Riverside Church in New York, once said that when a preacher tackles a controversial issue it is important to make it clear that the sermon is an invitation to dialogue. I think Coffin's comment is a good model for us all. The church, the Christian faith, has always had some issue or other boiling away on the stove of controversy. And, by the grace of God, we have often (although, not always) demonstrated that it *is* possible to have faithful dialogue and to cling to each other despite our differences. We do this in the belief that it is the Holy Spirit who binds us to each other, and not some other flimsy and transient thing—like human agreement on a hot-button issue that may be a non-issue a hundred years from now. In other words, my intention here is not to hand out a pronouncement of Trinity [Church]'s official stance (as if you would accept such a declaration in the first place), but to start a family conversation.

So, here goes. . . .

The Preacher's Stand. The immediate next line in the sermon is "I support the idea of gay marriage." Black Johnston elaborates by telling of his own life experiences that have played a key role in changing his perspective over the years. He also acknowledges that "experience alone is a one-legged stool. . . . It requires other revelatory legs—the legs of scripture, reason, and tradition—to provide a stable ethical and moral platform."

Black Johnston then discusses his own views regarding Scripture, the history of gay people in the life of the church ("Many of these historical people, including canonized saints, have been involved in lasting, committed relationships"), and current scientific research regarding whether sexual orientation is genetically determined or is a choice.

The Invitation Reissued

OK, I said that I wanted to contribute my two cents to a family conversation about these issues. I hope I have done so in a respectful manner, and I know that you all will get back to me with opinions of your own.

Linkage of the Issue with Infant Baptism. After acknowledging that some in the congregation are probably embarrassed that he is preaching about same-sex marriage on a day when a baby will be baptized, Black Johnston also reminds the church of its promises to care for the child, to raise it up in the faith, and to welcome that child into the community of faith:

We pronounce God's blessings on that child. When do we decide that a child is no longer fit to receive God's blessing? . . . While the church may withhold its blessing from [same-sex relationships], I believe that God does not.

Conclusion

> In the hopes that God will always foster holy conversations in this
> community, let us stand together and confess our faith, using the
> words of the Confession of 1967....

2. Problem—Resolution—New Possibility

One of the classic ways to preach on a particular topic or issue—including a controversial social issue—is through a problem–resolution–new
possibility form. The preacher begins by explicating the problem at
hand, its causes, and the challenges it poses for contemporary hearers.
The preacher then turns to the Bible and theology for the solution to
the problem. Finally, the preacher moves to a place in which he or she
envisions new possibilities for living in light of the new perspective
given to the problem through biblical and theological reflection.

In the sermon that follows Episcopal priest Whitney Rice identifies
in her introduction the problem she will address: namely, racism against
Native Americans. She then proceeds through narrative, statistical evidence, and appeal to popular culture to flesh out the problem. Finally,
through creative use of the biblical text about Cain and Abel, she offers a
theological perspective on the problem (a resolution of sorts), and invites
her hearers to participate in the new possibilities God intends.

Whitney Rice, "The Blood That Cries Out from the Ground"[4] (Genesis 4:1–16)

Introduction. When we think of the word "racism" we often think of
words like "discrimination, Jim Crow laws, Martin Luther King, Jr., Ku
Klux Klan, Uncle Tom and Aunt Jemima, segregation." We don't often
think of words like "reservation, Indian giver, gambling, cowboys and
Indians, Crazy Horse Malt Liquor, Jeep Cherokee and Dodge Dakota,
redskin." Yet Native American racism is a major problem for our nation.

The Problem. Rice tells a story about a class she took in American Indian
literature as a college student in Kansas in which she learned about the
way Christian missionaries in that state had kidnapped Indian children
and forced them to live apart from their families at a boarding school.
She concludes with the story of how an eleven-year-old girl and her

two-year-old sister, both of whom were residents of the school, froze to death while trying to find their way back to their Ojibwe tribe in Minnesota. The school never even notified the girls' parents of their deaths. She likens this to the story of Cain and Abel in which the Lord says to Cain, "What have you done? Listen, your brother's blood is crying out to me from the ground! And now you are cursed from the ground, which has opened its mouth to receive your brother's blood from your hand" (Gen. 4:10–11).

Rice then gives statistical facts about the plight of Native Americans, culminating with a poem written by a Coeur d'Alene tribal member called "Hunger Psalm: 1973."

The Resolution. Rice returns to the story of Cain and Abel, reminding her hearers that God "will not let Cain sink into suicidal despair, just waiting for someone to kill him and end his torturous guilt" but instead puts a mark on him so that "no one who came upon him would kill him" and then sends him into the Land of Nod, which means Land of Wandering:

> We [Americans] are wandering with Cain, lost in disgrace. . . . We are somewhere east of Eden, and it is a dark and desperate place.
>
> But does God keep us alive simply to punish us? No. God sustains our lives so that we might learn and grow, repent and be forgiven, change and be redeemed.

The New Possibility. Rice names a number of positive actions her hearers can take in response to God's grace, including "a heightened awareness of the pejorative way American Indians are portrayed in our culture," advocacy for AIM (the American Indian Movement), and a refusal to fall prey to generalizing stereotypes.

Conclusion

> God is not afraid of our fear . . . , and God is not defeated by our despair. But God is hurt by our pain. . . . God hears blood crying out from the ground, the blood of Abel and the blood of two little girls running away. . . . We can honor that blood by working to bring the Kingdom of God on earth, which we will know when "mercy and truth are met together, righteousness and peace have kissed each other" (Ps. 85:10, paraphrase).

3. Narrative Structure: My Story, the Biblical Story, Our Story

In *Preaching the Story,* Lutheran homiletician Edmund Steimle outlines a narrative form for preaching that begins with the preacher's own story (something the preacher has experienced or observed), moves to the biblical story (a retelling of what was going on in the biblical text, along with theological affirmations growing out of it), and then moves to "our" story—that is, the congregation's story, and how the biblical text influences it.[5] This form is useful for many types of preaching, including prophetic preaching. Barbara Lundblad, professor of homiletics at Union Theological Seminary in New York, demonstrates its potential well in her sermon "No Small Thing."

Barbara Lundblad, "No Small Thing"[6] (1 Samuel 20:12–23, 35–42)

My (The Preacher's) Story. Lundblad tells the story of two fifth-grade girls who came running up to her after a worship service to say that they had become blood sisters under the maple tree in the Johnsons' backyard. She comments that "they had not yet learned that girls shouldn't show too much affection for one another."[7]

The Biblical Story. Lundblad tells the story of David and Jonathan who were friends in childhood, and how the bonds of their friendships were strong and passionate.

> The God of creation is a passionate God. . . . passion—not procreation—is uniquely human among God's gifts. While procreation is indeed a gift, it is given to giraffes and gerbils as well as to human beings. But passion, in all its fullness, goes beyond the mating cycles and is not bound by the need to reproduce ourselves.
>
> The story of David and Jonathan is a very passionate story. . . .[8]
>
> This is a story not only of passion but also of promise. . . . After Jonathan's death in battle, David takes Jonathan's crippled son into his own household. They become family though they are not related.[9]

Lundblad also cites two other biblical stories that exhibit such passion and promise in commitments that are made beyond bloodlines: the story of Ruth and Naomi, and the story of Jesus on the cross giving his mother Mary and the beloved disciples to one another as family.[10]

Our Story (Implications for Today's Hearers). Lundblad offers contemporary examples of where she sees such passion and vows incarnate today: A man whose life has been tragic befriends a woman who is going blind too early, and a middle-aged gay man visits his partner of many years in the hospital each day.

Conclusion

> Help us this day to cry, to laugh, to embrace, and to say, "I love you" to a friend. Help us to know that this, too, is a promise and a passion born of God.[11]

4. Thesis—Antithesis—Synthesis

In his book *The Certain Sound of the Trumpet,* Samuel Proctor advocates using a thesis-antithesis-synthesis structure in preaching. This sermon form follows a Hegelian dialectical model in shaping a sermon. Ronald Allen summarizes the movement in this model for preaching by noting that it begins with a thesis ("an interpretation of an aspect of God, the Bible, and the world"), then moves to the antithesis (the reasons that the opening interpretation cannot be completely correct), and finally to the synthesis (which mediates between the two by identifying points at which the thesis is true and also needs to be reshaped).[12] We see the form demonstrated in the following sermon by Martin Luther King Jr.

Martin Luther King Jr., "How Should a Christian View Communism?"[13] (Amos 5:24)

Introduction. King begins by stating at least three reasons every Christian minister should feel obligated to speak on the topic of Communism: (1) "the widespread influence of Communism," (2) the fact that "Communism is Christianity's most formidable rival," and (3) the reality that "it is unfair to condemn a system before we know what that system teaches and why it is wrong."[14]

Statement of the Thesis

Communism and Christianity are fundamentally incompatible.[15]

Arguments in Support of the Thesis

1. Communism has a "materialistic and humanistic view of life and history," and its atheism "provides no place for God or Christ."[16]
2. Communism "is based on ethical relativism and accepts no stable moral absolutes."[17] It uses any ends to achieve its means.
3. "Communism attributes ultimate value to the state."[18]
4. Communism ultimately robs humanity of freedom and ends up leaving human beings as "little more than a depersonalized cog in the ever-turning wheel of the state."[19]

Statement of the Antithesis

Yet something in the spirit and threat of Communism challenges us. The late Archbishop of Canterbury, William Temple, referred to Communism as a Christian heresy. He meant that Communism had laid hold on certain truths which are essential parts of the Christian view of things, although bound to them are theories and practices which no Christian could ever accept.[20]

Arguments in Support of the Antithesis

1. Communism challenges the church—which has not been true to its social mission, especially regarding racial justice—to be more concerned about social justice. Jesus champions the cause of the poor, the exploited, and the disinherited.[21]
2. Communism presses us to "examine honestly the weaknesses of traditional capitalism."[22]

Statement of the Synthesis

The Kingdom of God is neither the thesis of individual enterprise nor the antithesis of collective enterprise, but a synthesis which reconciles the truth of both.[23]

Conclusion

These are days when Christians must evince wise restraint and calm reasonableness. We must not call everyone a Communist or an appeaser who recognizes that hate and hysteria are not the final answers to the problems of these turbulent days. We must not engage in a negative anti-Communism, but rather a positive thrust for democracy, realizing that our greatest defense against Communism is to take offensive action in behalf of justice and righteousness.[24]

5. Structure around an Image

One compelling way to structure a sermon is around an image (or series of images). The image might be drawn from the biblical text or from contemporary life, and it often serves as a bridge between the two. One of the values of images is that they appeal to the senses and engage the hearer through sight, sound, touch, taste, or smell. In the first sermon below, Sheila Nelson-McJilton uses an image taken from Matthew 15:21–28, about the "crumbs" the Canaanite woman seeks from Jesus. Nelson-McJilton uses this image as a metaphor for contrasting our desires and those of the poor. In the second sermon, Veronica Goines uses the image of the neck bone—a piece of chicken that she watched her relatives eat with relish at family gatherings—as a symbol of the resilience and creativity of her African American ancestors who "by grace, possess the faith to receive the scraps of this world and create a feast."

Sheila Nelson-McJilton, "Crumbs"[25] (Matthew 15:21–28)

Introduction of the Image. A woman comes to Jesus seeking crumbs, healing for her daughter. When met with the silence and rebuke of the disciples, she exhibits "the kind of fierce, ferocious faith that will transform a world." Out of that faith, "the woman receives what she demands. Healing for her daughter. Mercy that is wide and broad and wonderfully kind and faithful and bountiful."[26]

The Image as Related to Us. Because we have claimed places at God's table, we have a responsibility to feed our brothers and sisters.

> Crumbs. That's all they are looking for. Crumbs. Not the whole loaf. Not even a slice. Just crumbs. You and I want the whole loaf, of course, and we usually get it. We drive SUVs. They take buses or the subway, or they walk. We have pension plans. They lack basic health insurance so they must bring crying babies to the emergency room at midnight. We have two-hundred-thousand-dollar homes with two-car garages. They live in crowded, noisy apartments. . . .

Crumbs. They want more than crumbs because deep in their souls, they know they deserve more. And yet they often do not know who to ask or how to ask. So they wait. . . .

Will you feed them?[27]

Conclusion (with Image Reiterated). In Christ and through Christ, we are all worthy to come to God's banquet table, and no one gets crumbs here. God's table is full of big, crusty, homemade loaves of bread. It is full of rich, red wine. The gifts of God for the people of God.[28]

Veronica Goines, "Neckbone Faith"[29] (Jeremiah 17:5–10; Luke 6:17–26)

Introduction of the Image. When Goines was a child, she and her extended family would gather after church on Sundays for a traditional soul-food meal. Inevitably her parents and other adult relatives would ask for and enjoy the neck bone of the chicken, and she could never understand why.

But I have come to realize that neck bones are a metaphor for the experience of African Americans and for all people who, by grace, possess the faith to receive the scraps of this world and create a feast. . . . Anyone can make a feast of a filet mignon. But a neck bone? Well, that's an occasion for a new vision. It is a vision of blessings.[30]

Development of the Image

Slaves, who had very little, often used the leftovers they had to form something new. . . . When given rags, the women formed quilting bees. When given ham bones, they fed whole communities. . . and from neck bones came rich and savory stock in which to cook greens, black-eyed peas, soups, stuffing, stews, gravy and much more. . . . Through the common experience of suffering, in the depths of oppression and slavery, emerged a faith and generosity that was the source of life, joy, creativity, nourishment, community, and blessing.[31]

Goines then tells how the slaves also created their own faith practices through creative use of the remnants of the faith that were not tainted for them by their white masters. They memorized Scripture, preached in the "invisible church," sang subversive spirituals, and "facilitated a common and transcendent experience of worship—spontaneous and extemporaneous, born of Holy Spirit power and every deep human emotion, embodied memory and present reality."[32] While they had every right to be depressed, they were resilient instead.

> Like trees planted by the rivers of water they yielded the fruit of resilience and strength; as co-creators with God, they brought life out of chaos, light out of darkness, and hope out of despair.[33]

Other Contemporary Embodiments of the Image

> You may have parents who survived the Holocaust or the Japanese internment camps of World War II. Maybe your great-grandparents lived through the horrors of slavery. Or perhaps you are a present-day refugee of the Sudan, Haiti, or Hurricane Katrina. You may be living with catastrophic illness. It takes an overcoming faith to bring you through such realities. Neck bone faith emerges out of dire circumstances, with power to transform those circumstances.[34]

Conclusion (with Image Reiterated)

> Come the last Sunday in February, I will stand in the buffet line at the soul food feast and say to the servers, "I'd like some neck bones, please." . . . I will acknowledge my parents and ancestors, who taught me well how to hold to God's unchanging hand, to receive the scraps of this world and create a feast, to perceive the goodness of God in the midst of adversity, and to hear the blessings of Jesus above the curses of this world.[35]

6. Letter Form

While letter writing is certainly an ancient literary form, it is not always considered to be a potential sermon form. Yet if we think about it, the early letters of the apostles to the first Christian churches were one of the most common forms of preaching in the earliest days of Christianity. Believers gathered on the Lord's Day and heard those letters read aloud in worship—giving them instruction, hope, and encouragement for their lives in Christ.

Below we consider two preachers who also used letter forms in their prophetic proclamation. In the first example, Martin Luther King Jr. preaches a sermon in which the form is an imaginary letter from the apostle Paul to American Christians living in the mid-twentieth century.

In the second example, Ernest Campbell, pastor of The Riverside Church in New York City from 1968 to 1976, uses the letter form in a very different way. He writes a letter to evangelist Billy Graham, taking him to task for his refusal to serve as a prophet to Richard Nixon during the days of the Vietnam War, and he invites his congregation to "overhear" the prophetic word he proclaims within it.

Martin Luther King Jr., "Paul's Letter to American Christians"[36]

Salutation and Greeting

> I, an apostle of Jesus Christ, by the will of God, to you who are in America, grace and peace be unto you through our Lord and Savior, Jesus Christ.[37]

Body of Letter

> For many years I have longed to be able to come to see you. I have heard so much of you and what you are doing.[38]

King then cites scientific, technological, and medical advances that have been made by Americans.

> But, America, as I look at you from afar, I wonder whether your moral and spiritual progress has been commensurate with your scientific progress.[39]

King (in the name of Paul) goes on to name such evils as the unmitigated desire for social acceptance, the misuse of capitalism for ungodly ends, and the segregation of the body of Christ.[40]

King calls on Americans to remember his advice given in his letter to the Romans:

> Be ye not conformed to this world; but be ye transformed by the renewing of your mind [Rom. 12:2 KJV].
>
> You have a dual citizenry. You live in both time and eternity, both in heaven and earth. Therefore your ultimate allegiance is not to the

government, not to the state, not to the nation, not to any man-made institution. The Christian owes his ultimate allegiance to God . . . .[41]

He also calls them to do their part in ending segregation and to remember that "the highest good is love."[42] In an eloquent rephrasing of 1 Corinthians 13, he writes,

> So American Christians, you may master the intricacies of the English language. You may possess all the eloquence of articulate speech. . . .
> You may have the gift of prophecy and understand all mysteries. . . . You may ascend to the heights of academic achievement, so that you have all knowledge. . . you may give your goods to feed the poor. . . . You may tower high in philanthropy, but if you have not love, it means nothing. . . .[43]

Closing

> I hope this letter finds you strong in faith. It may be that I will not get to see you in America, but I will meet you in God's eternity.[44]

Ernest T. Campbell, "An Open Letter to Billy Graham"[45]

Introduction. Campbell announces that he will use a sermon form he has never before used in his twenty-five years of ministry: an open letter. His desire is to address himself "not so much to Billy Graham the man, as to the position he represents in the religious life of America."[46] He also tells the congregation that he forwarded a copy of his letter to Graham by airmail before preaching it.

Salutation and Greetings. Campbell greets Graham "in the name of our Lord and Savior Jesus Christ."[47] He acknowledges similarities in their backgrounds (since Campbell and Graham attended the same college and Campbell shared many of Graham's theological views in his younger years), names a time and place where the two had met, and mentions mutual friends. He also commends Graham for his "remarkable durability and fiscal integrity"[48] and his composure under fire.

Body of the Letter. Campbell says that the immediate provocation for his letter is Graham's failure to respond to a telegram from a leader of Key '73, urging Graham to use his influence with President Nixon and to urge Nixon to cease all bombing in Vietnam. Campbell considers five possible reasons for Graham's lack of response:

1. You did not receive the message. . . .
2. You received the message and made some unreported effort to influence the president to stop the bombing. . . .
3. You received the message and did not agree with its agonizing appraisal of the bombing. . . .
4. You received the message and agree with its general intent but fear that any forthright declaration you might make would jeopardize your connections with the Establishment. . . .
5. You received the message, sympathized with its basic sentiment, but lacked a theological rationale for speaking out. . . .[49]

Then Campbell argues his case for why Graham should speak out: History matters for Christians, he says, and God works within history to bring about just purposes; "those who disavow social action as a proper expression of Christian faith become . . . advocates of the status quo";[50] "morality" has to do not only with personal integrity, but with issues related to the making of war, poverty, homelessness, and other justice concerns; and certain portions of Scripture call for social action (such as Mary's Magnificat and the final judgment scene in Matthew 25).[51]

Campbell then encourages Graham to be a leader who breaks down the dividing walls between the evangelical and social action camps by embracing a fuller understanding of evangelicalism that goes hand in hand with social activism.

Closing. Campbell invites Graham to preach at Riverside Church in response to the issues and questions raised in his letter and also urges him to receive the letter in "the spirit of openness and genuine concern." He concludes with these lines: "The stakes are high. The time is short, the nation is badly torn. Is there no balm in Gilead? Why then is the health of our people not recovered?"[52]

7. Action Structure: Biblical Models, Areas Needing Action, and Call to Action

The Bible tells many stories of people who engaged in actions on behalf of justice. The preacher can structure a sermon that draws analogies between the actions for justice in biblical times and those that are needed today, as Walter Burghardt does in the following sermon.

Walter Burghardt, "God's Justice and America's Sixth Child"[53] (Deuteronomy 15:7–11; Mark 9:35–37; 10:13–15)

Two Biblical Models for Action. The sermon begins by talking about two biblical characters: Joshua, who felled Jericho after walking around its walls for six days; and the persistent widow in Luke's Gospel who pounds on the judge's door until justice is granted. Both are consumed by "justice" as Scripture defines it: loving God above all, loving neighbor as self, and treating the earth with reverence and respect.[54]

Two Justice Issues Today That Call for Action. Burghardt names violence and health care as two justice issues that call for action today. As examples, he cites grim statistics on violence and the victimization of children in the United States and statistics on our nation's poor showing in relation to the rest of the world in providing health care for children.

Call to Action

> We are called to be Joshua and the Widow today. "When you are raising your voices for your children, *you are not on your knees begging for charity*. Your heads held high, *you are demanding justice*."[55]
>
> A priority for the poor is not on the U.S. political agenda today, and we are called to march "around our nation's capitol seven times, as Andy Young did in the 1960s, clamoring with all the passion of the widow, 'Justice, Give us Justice! Justice for these children of God!'"[56]

8. Socratic Teaching Sermon (Moving from Questions to Answers)

Prophetic sermons can also be teaching sermons, in which the preacher takes key questions the parishioners are asking about an issue of concern and addresses them theologically. The sermon outlined next addresses theological questions raised in light of the Re-imagining Conference held in Minneapolis in 1993 and attended by women from several Christian denominations. The conference provoked much controversy in church presses, with some charging its participants with heresy for how they re-imagined God. Ronald Allen, professor of preaching at Christian Theological Seminary in Indianapolis, addressed some of the most controversial issues raised at the conference in his sermon "Come, Sophia."

Ronald J. Allen, "Come, Sophia"[57] (Proverbs 1, 8, 9)

Introduction. The sermon begins by acknowledging the angry and concerned responses in Allen's congregation to the Re-imagining Conference. Among the questions raised are "Where did the word *Sophia* originate?" "What does it mean?" "Why was it used at a Christian meeting?" "Did the conference engage in goddess worship when it invoked Sophia?"

Body. The body of the sermon addresses each question in turn, providing succinct but informed biblical and theological responses to the questions raised. Key theological affirmations include "Wisdom is not God. But she is in as close a proximity to God as any created thing can be."[58] She helped create the world and mediates God's presence and purposes. Christ is spoken of in the New Testament as the "wisdom" and power of God. God transcends male and female, but "Sophia can help us appreciate how women's lives can deepen our understanding of God."[59]

Conclusion. Ron Allen tells the story of how he had a large ugly birthmark on his head as a child, and of the taunting he received from other children. On one occasion his mother wrapped his sobbing body in her apron and mediated God's presence to him. "That day I called her Mother. Today I might call her Sophia."[60]

9. Play on Words

There are occasions when the tensions that exist between words—whether within a biblical text, between several texts, or between the text and contemporary life—allow the preacher the opportunity to engage in sermonic wordplay. Such tension or contradictions not only allow the preacher to name reality in a more holistic and complex way; they can also lead to deeper truths about the gospel itself.

Early in my teaching career I was invited to preach for the annual lecture and reunion week at Union Theological Seminary in Virginia, where I was then on the faculty. I remember being at a loss for how to begin thinking about the sermon, so I turned to the daily lectionary passages for the day to see if they would give me any ideas. The Old Testament text for the day was from Isaiah, where the prophet exclaims,

> "How beautiful upon the mountains
> are the feet of the messenger who announces peace."
> (Isa. 52:7)

The New Testament lesson was a passage from Galatians in which Paul speaks of having "labor pains" because of the refusal of the Galatians to embrace the gospel he is proclaiming in their midst (Gal. 4:19). As I pondered those two words and the two images, the sermon took shape around them.[61] "Beautiful feet" came to represent those times in ministry when people think we are wonderful and can only see good in us. "Labor pains" came to represent those times in ministry when we preach the prophetic gospel of God and experience strong resistance to its embrace. I concluded the sermon by saying that the reality of ministry is that if we are preaching the whole two-edged gospel, we will have days when people think our feet are beautiful and days when the sermon feels like a breech birth. But faithfulness to God and to the gospel requires that we do no less.

Teresa Fry Brown, "Justice or Just Us?"[62]

In her sermon "Justice or Just Us?" Teresa Fry Brown engages in wordplay as well. Only in this instance she contrasts the prophet Micah's call to "do justice" (Mic. 6:8) with our human proclivity to focus instead on "just us."

Introduction. Fry Brown begins by asking her hearers if they can feel, see, taste, and smell injustice in their midst. She names a number of instances of injustice:

Denominational elitism signifying God's favor for some and disdain for others.

Militaristic budgetary priorities while millions of children go to bed hungry.

Recidivism of gender attitudes seeking the return of Victorian values and the rebuilding of a man's castle.

Generational discrimination evidenced in media presentations of youth culture and the expendability of elders.

Death from diseases only "those people" contract . . . *Are we doing justice or just us?*

God's Desire for Justice

Though people were worshiping other gods in Micah's time (including money, position, power, elitism, ethnocentrism), God called them to justice and equality for all people.

Justice is not a denominational program,

A racial, ethnic privilege,

A gender-based prerogative.

It is a God-ordained imperative.

[It is] not based on guilt, moralism, or a misguided obedience to a principle of political correctness [but is] a joyful, festive response to God's in-breaking in the future.

Justice or Just Us? Fry Brown gives several lists of what "Just Us" looks like ("we-they, us-them, those young people . . . old people . . . gays . . . straights . . . rich . . . poor") and concludes with the words "Just Us is a stagnant, corroded, immobile faith."

By contrast, she says, to do justice means to "risk humiliation . . . risk our lives . . . risk joy."

The Spirit's Anointing for Justice

The Spirit has called us to do justice, and will empower us to heal the brokenhearted, preach good news to the poor, announce pardon to prisoners, set the burdened and battered free, and announce, "This is God's year to act!" "God will empower us if we are willing to do JUSTICE AND NOT JUST US!"

10. Upsetting the Equilibrium (Moving from Ease to Dis-Ease)

In his book *The Homiletical Plot,* Eugene Lowry sets forth a narrative model for preaching in which the preacher moves from upsetting the equilibrium to some sort of resolution of the sermon's initial tension.[63]

However, sometimes in prophetic preaching, the movement in a sermon may be all about upsetting the equilibrium—and leaving it that way. The prophet's role is to shake us out of our "ease" and into a state of "dis-ease" so that we see ourselves and our calling in Christ differently.

Brian K. Blount, "God on the Loose"[64] (Mark 1:9–11)

Introduction: The Birth of Kaylin Blount. Brian Blount begins his sermon by telling the story of his daughter Kaylin's birth: about the way she tore into the world, taking charge of everything she surveyed and literally bringing her professor father to his knees (as he tried to crawl out of the room so she would stay asleep). "A mind bending, life-altering, change your ways kind of force had gotten loose and was running amok in our lives."[65]

Biblical Story: God Breaks into the World and Is "On the Loose" through the Baptism of Jesus

> Clouds tearing. Heavens ripping. Divine voice booming. Spirit descending. This is terrible, untamed Tiger talk. It is the language of slashing and slicing, shredding and clawing, until something once locked up on that safe and seldom seen heavenly side over there knifes its way free to this historical, human side we're standing on over here.[66]

And God's appearance was strange!

> It's like, you're looking for God in a great building with long halls, high ceilings, a magnificent steeple, dressed in a long robe, most likely with doctor's stripes on the sleeves . . . and then God comes sliding out of some trailer park, hanging out with people from the wrong side of the tracks.[67]

And it gets stranger still. The Spirit of God possesses Jesus, and from then on, he's in big trouble with all he encounters.

> When God gets into you, you get into trouble, because God *drives* you until you're running wild in a world hell bent on religiously remaining its same, tame, shameful self.[68]

The Troubling Call to Us: To Be Leaders Who Welcome God on the Loose

We might as well admit it. We don't *really* want a wild God on the loose. Not in our world. Certainly not in our churches. Not really. Especially not in church where we want everything just so. We really want a domesticated God, a charismatic but captivated cat, a holy, but humbled hound dog. We want the power that God and God's reign represent, but we want that power domesticated, working for us. We want it on a leash. Our leash.

But Jesus' story of baptism suggests that this is not how God works. When God gets hold of us God drives us to where God wants us to go, to what God wants us to do, not where we'd rather be, or what we'd rather not do.[69]

The Good News in the Midst of the Troubling News

But that's the good news! There's good news whenever boundaries are broken down, buffers are ripped apart, dividing lines are shredded, and people are set free to reach out to others and set them free too. The good news in this story about God breaking free into Jesus and Jesus breaking free into our world is that we can tap into that boundary-breaking power to change the world in which we live. That is a kind of Tiger that it's *good* to have on the loose, running free and unfettered.[70]

11. Invitation to Lament

There are occasions when the grief of a community, a nation, or the world is so great that the sermon's appropriate role is to invite the congregation into a place of mourning and weeping in solidarity with those who are suffering. To do so is not to deny the hope that is at the heart of the gospel. Rather, it is to acknowledge that lament rightly belongs in worship and that sometimes the hope for which we long is proclaimed through hymns, prayers, sacraments, and other liturgical elements that surround and encompass the preaching event. The sermon doesn't have to do it all.

In the sermon that follows, preached during a daily chapel service at

Yale Divinity School two weeks after Hurricane Katrina had brought devastation to the Gulf Coast of the United States, biblical scholar Carolyn Sharp invites the gathered community to join in Rachel's lament over the brokenness of our world and to "refuse to be consoled" until justice finally comes.

Carolyn J. Sharp, "Refuse to Be Consoled"[71]
(Psalm 50; Philippians 2:12–20; Matthew 2:13–23)

Introduction

> Crises of the spirit can take many different forms as we struggle to work through them and seek God in them. . . . I am in a place of crisis this morning. I would invite you to stay present with me in this discomfort as we reflect on the spiritual crisis into which many of us have been thrown by the catastrophe in the Gulf Coast.

Hearing the Lament of the World

> We have heard the voice of Rachel weeping this past week, haven't we? As if our ears and eyes had not been filled enough with the sounds and sights of death: civil warfare and disease in Africa, the war in Iraq, the tsunami of last December. The devastation of the Gulf Coast has inundated us with new images of suffering, people sobbing, struggling, and raging against the failure of imagination that has hobbled our relief efforts in the wake of Hurricane Katrina.

Sharp acknowledges the blessings and graces of the relief efforts but also confesses to being overwhelmed by the images of pain and confusion that have been broadcast night after night.

> The insistence of this news coverage has shown me with a chilling clarity what we don't usually see—how easily we forget the suffering of the world's poor.

Acknowledging Our Complicity in the Suffering

> I wish I could just put all the blame on FEMA, on governmental inefficiency, but I can't do that with integrity. I reach for Scripture, but there is no easy hope there either.

Invitation to Lament

> I can't end that way [with easy hope]. So instead, I invite you to hear
> these Gospel words and mark them as holy: "Rachel weeping for her
> children, *refusing to be consoled,* because they are no more" [Matt.
> 2:18b]. Mark as holy her refusal to be consoled at the suffering and
> death of the innocent whom she loved, and let us likewise stay pres-
> ent to the suffering and death of those who are beloved of God.

Sharp then names ways in which her hearers should refuse to be consoled over the suffering in New Orleans, the Congo, Iraq, Afghanistan,
Haiti, and Harlem.

Conclusion

> For the love of God, refuse to be consoled. Instead offer to God the
> spiritual sacrifice of your passion for justice, your compassion for
> those who suffer—and seek to be instruments of God's justice and
> reconciling love.

Susan Durber, "The Massacre of the Innocents"[72] (Matthew 2:1–18)

In a sermon she preached on the first Sunday of Epiphany, a Sunday
in which the Gospel lectionary text for the day was the slaughter of the
innocents in Matthew 2, British pastor Susan Durber also invited her
congregation to lament, this time over the violent deaths of innocent
children that are still taking place in our world today. Her sermon cen-
ters around a retelling of the story of the advent of the wise men by a
woman who lost her children to Herod's terror.

Introduction. Durber first invites her hearers to think back to Christmas cards they have received and to envision the photos on them. She
then acknowledges that she has never received a card featuring a photo
of the massacre of the children described in Matthew 2:1–18. Yet the
massacre of children still goes on, Durber tells the congregation, and
she names specific instances of that slaughter in her own particular context and in the global context. She then challenges the notion that faith
should be a place where "everything horrible is cut out and where we
forget for a moment the shades and the pain. . . . When we have faced
the depths, we know what it is to grasp for deliverance."[73]

Retelling the Biblical Story from a New Vantage Point. Durber insists that although we tend to separate the story of the wise men coming with gifts to see baby Jesus from the story of the slaughter of the innocents, they are really one story. She invites her congregation to hear again the old, familiar story as she imaginatively tells it from a new vantage point—that of a nameless mother who has watched one of Herod's soldiers slit the throats of her two young male children. This mother, in her anguish and anger, takes on the notion that the magi were "wise."

> "You stopped to call on Herod to exchange compliments. Didn't you realize that it does no good to pay compliments to tyrants, that you were wasting your time and risking our lives? I do not forgive your naiveté or think you are innocent. . . . The blood of our sons is on your hands. You are not my kind." [74]

Theological Affirmation: God Suffers with Us. Durber asks how we can respond to the mothers and fathers who have lost their children.

> Does it look to them as though God in the Bible story escaped the pain of the slaughter? The Jesus child has all the luck of the gods and leaves behind the real suffering, fleeing into Egypt. Did Mary ever look back on the suffering town and feel guilty that her son had escaped the killing? And did she think of that moment as she held the body of her son on Calvary, as they lifted him down from the cross? Our faith tells us that God does not escape the pain—that God is as close as our own breathing with those who suffer. . . .
>
> We do have something to say . . . to all those who have faced life at its bitterest. God is with us. God is with us.[75]

Conclusion. Durber ends her sermon with a second retelling of the story—this time beginning with the visit of the magi who "wept with joy to see God in the face of a baby," and ending with the slaughter of other babies when "there was room only for weeping and for grief."[76]

> And they came for Mary's child and killed him, piercing his body with a spear. Mary wept for her child. The wise women embraced her, but she would not be comforted. And a voice was heard in Ramah,

sobbing in bitter grief; it was God weeping for her children, refusing to be comforted.[77]

12. Confessional: "Here I Stand"

Finally, it is important to acknowledge that sometimes prophetic sermons are preached as much for the pastor as for the congregation—especially on occasions when the pastor needs to proclaim with Martin Luther, "Here I stand." Perhaps the pastor senses a need to go on record publicly regarding a controversial issue or to come clean about a change of heart she or he has had. Whatever the case, the sermon in such instances often has the tone of confession as the preacher honestly and forthrightly professes what she or he believes, and perhaps also repents of past wrongs.

We see a prime example of such preaching in Harry Emerson Fosdick's eloquent sermon "The Unknown Soldier." In this sermon, preached on the weekend when tombs to the unknown soldier were being dedicated all over the world in honor of those who lost their lives in World War I, Fosdick proclaims his own stand as a pacifist and repents of ways in which he aided and abetted soldiers during the Great War.

Harry Emerson Fosdick, "The Unknown Soldier"[78]

Introduction. Fosdick begins the sermon by saying how strange it is that in great capitals of the world this weekend, the body of an unrecognized soldier will be dedicated with great military pageantry in homage to the Great War.

Confession

> You may say that I, being a Christian minister, did not know him. I knew him well. [79]

Fosdick tells how he spent months with the troops in Europe, urging soldiers on "for their suicidal and murderous endeavor" and sending them into battle with prayers and hymns. Three times he wonders aloud if the Unknown Soldier was among the groups that he, a Christian minister, sent into battle.[80]

"This Is More about Me Than You"

> You here this morning may listen to the rest of this sermon or not, as you please. It makes much less difference to me than usual what you do or think. I have an account to settle in this pulpit today between my soul and the Unknown Soldier.[81]

The Case for Pacifism. Fosdick spends most of his sermon focusing on the absurdity of war, the cost of war, the lack of glory in war, the fact that war never ends war, the horrors war inflicts on its victims (both on soldiers and on those they fight against), and the ways in which war corrupts Christians and their ideals for its own purposes.

Fosdick calls on the church to stay out of war and to withdraw from every alliance that encourages it.

Conclusion: "Here I Stand"

> I renounce war. I renounce war because of what it does to our men. I have seen the long, long hospital trains filled with their mutilated bodies. I have heard the cries of the crazed and the prayers of those who wanted to die and could not, and I remember the maimed and ruined men for whom the war is not yet over. I renounce war because of what it compels us to do to our enemies, bombing their mothers in villages, starving their children by blockades, laughing over our coffee cups about every damnable thing we have been able to do to them. I renounce war for its consequences, for the lies it lives on and propagates, for the undying hatreds it arouses, for the dictatorships it puts in the place of democracy, for the starvation that stalks after it. I renounce war and never again, directly or indirectly, will I sanction or support another! O Unknown Soldier, in penitent reparation I make you that pledge.[82]

CONCLUSION

Sometimes prophetic preaching is caricatured as being nonbiblical (and overly political) in content, strident in tone, and confrontational in address. Yet as the examples given in this chapter evidence, prophetic preaching can be as varied in content, form, and tone as any other kind of Christian preaching. The sermon can begin with a biblical text, a narrative from everyday life, an image, or a problem to be pondered. It can lead people to weep, to think more critically, to see the world with new eyes, or to engage in advocacy or action. Its tone can be invitational, confessional, provocative, or inspirational. What is important (for this book's concerns, at least) is that the prophetic preacher engage a sermon form that exhibits pastoral sensitivity for the congregation while also clearly communicating the intended message. The good news is that the options for doing so are manifold!

5

Word and *Deed:*
The Integrity of Prophetic Witness

God doesn't require us to succeed; [God] only requires that you try.
                                                                    Mother Teresa

To be a Christian is to live dangerously, honestly, freely—to step in
the name of love as if you may land on nothing, yet to keep stepping
because the something that sustains you no empire can give you and no
empire take away.[1]
                                                    Cornel West, *Democracy Matters*

Early in my ministry I had the privilege of working with one of my
former seminary professors on a paper our presbytery was considering
adopting that called for a simplicity of lifestyle among Christians (or,
as the slogan of the times went, "Living simply so that others might
simply live"). After we had presented the first draft of the paper, yet
before its final approval, my professor told me that he had been to see
the president of the seminary where he taught and had asked the president to put a freeze on any more salary increases for him in the future.
I looked at him, somewhat astonished by what he had done (for I knew
that he was battling serious illness and that his family could definitely
use the additional income), and he responded by saying, "Nora, you
don't think you can just talk about this stuff and not have it change
your life, do you?"

If truth be told, his words have haunted me through the years,
because I sometimes prefer to live under the illusion that it is possible
to speak about critical issues of the day from the pulpit without having
that Word of God also require dramatic changes of me and my lifestyle. Yet I also have to admit that the prophets whose words have most
influenced my own life have been people whose deeds have gone hand
in hand with their words.

I remember, for example, the powerful witness of those scholars
and pastors and poets in South Korea in the 1970s who were impris-
oned and tortured because of their acts of protest against the dictatorial

regime of then-president Park Chung Hee. I think of pastors I knew during the Vietnam War era who lost their pulpits because of their outspokenness against that war. I think of the freedom riders and lunch-counter sit-in participants who risked ridicule, physical harm, and imprisonment during the civil rights era in order to witness to the truths in which they believed. And I think of the seminary students I have taught through the years who have inspired and challenged me through their sacrificial witness of advocacy and action on behalf of the poor and the dispossessed.

If truth be told, one of the most unnerving things about prophetic witness is that it often requires the prophet to put his or her body on the line on behalf of the Word proclaimed. The biblical prophets certainly give testimony to this reality. Picture Jeremiah walking around Jerusalem for days with a heavy yoke upon his shoulders, Esther risking her life by appearing unannounced before the king of Persia, or John the Baptist awaiting the verdict of the king in his prison cell. Prophetic witness can be costly. Yet this very costliness also makes it part and parcel of the gospel Jesus came preaching and living: a gospel that repeatedly reminds us that it is only as we lose our lives for the gospel's sake that we find them.

In this final chapter, I reflect on the relationship between word and deed in prophetic witness. I do so with no small amount of trepidation because I know how difficult it is to put our bodies where our mouths are. Yet I also believe that if we are going to talk holistically about prophetic witness, we need to consider not only the words the preacher preaches and the sermons the congregation hears, but also the prophetic actions in which both preacher and congregations engage on behalf of God's justice in the world.

WORD AND DEED IN THE WITNESS OF THE PREACHER

Not long ago I gave a lecture on prophetic preaching to a group of pastors and then asked them to reflect on strategies they personally had used in prophetic preaching. They named a number of useful strategies and talked candidly about their strengths and weaknesses. At the break after the discussion, one of the pastors approached me and said, "If truth be told, I don't preach many prophetic sermons. But I do engage in prophetic acts on a fairly regular basis. In fact, my picture has been in our local small-town paper on more than one occasion in recent months because of my participation in antiwar protests. I suppose it's a tribute to my congregation that they haven't yet tried to run me out of town for it. But do you think that such actions can sometimes take the place of sermons?"

His question brought to mind the introductory preaching classes I teach each fall in which my faculty colleague and I ask the students to reflect on an outstanding preacher they have heard and to describe what makes him or her so. Inevitably their comments not only include reflections on the sermons they heard preached but also on that preacher's witness outside the pulpit—and the ways that witness embodied the preacher's message.

In his book *Where Have All the Prophets Gone?* Marvin McMickle insists that "*prophetic preaching* must flow out of *prophetic ministry*. It is not simply a matter of speech; it is a matter of the inter-connection of speech and action."[2] He writes,

> Moses did not simply speak against the policies of Pharaoh; he physically confronted Pharaoh with the words from God, "Let my people go." Amos did not speak against King Jeroboam from the safety of his home in Tekoa in Judea. Instead, he went to the court of Jeroboam in Bethel inside of the Northern Kingdom of Israel to make his point. Nathan did not talk behind David's back. Instead Nathan stood in the presence of the king and declared, "You are the man." . . .
>
> There is no prophetic preaching that is limited to words alone. The things about which the prophet is willing to speak must be the things about which the prophet is also prepared to act.[3]

Allan Boesak sounded a similar theme in a sermon he preached on the occasion of the dedication of the offices of the newly reunited Presbyterian Church (U.S.A.) in the mid 1980s. Boesak, a South African pastor who was known for his witness against apartheid, preached a sermon titled "Prophetic Faithfulness" in which he called on the newly reunited denomination to become a prophetic witness in the world.[4] But he also stretched then-current understandings of prophetic witness with these words:

> We think the church is prophetic when we make statements. We say when we go to assemblies, the church has been prophetic because we have this wonderful resolution on South Africa and sanctions or something.

That is not being prophetic. The church is not prophetic when we make a resolution or take a decision, or even when we write a memorandum that we send to Congress or the president. That is not prophetic witness.

We really become prophetic only when we take those words and those resolutions and the meaning that they have and we give them life with our bodies, with the risks we take, with the testimony we give, and with the witness we are in the world on the streets, so that people can see what it means to be the church. Only then are we prophetic.

My church has the Confession of Belhar, which is one of the most incredible documents that we have ever produced in our country. It is a beautiful document that says God is on the side of the poor. It says apartheid is heresy, and we thought we were prophetic when we said that. But we discovered that we became prophetic only when we were willing and able by God's grace to take courage and stand in the streets and say, "This is the Confession," and go to jail and say, "This is the Confession," and face the tear gas and the dogs and the guns and say, "This is the Confession of the church." Then, and then only, are we prophetic.[5]

It is the witness of prophets who have literally put their lives on the line for justice—prophets like Allan Boesak and Nelson Mandela and Desmond Tutu, prophets like Rosa Parks and Sojourner Truth and Martin Luther King Jr., prophets like Oscar Romero and the Mary-knoll sisters who lost their lives in El Salvador—who remind us that prophetic witness does not end with words. It often requires far more of the prophet, including actions that are bold, dangerous, and costly. But how do we become motivated to engage in such acts? What is it that compels and inspires us to do so?

In his challenge to pastors to take up the mantle of prophetic witness once again, Marvin McMickle paraphrases Cornel West's three-fold action agenda as a way of offering practical strategies for those who want to aim for a reintegration of word and deed in their own prophetic witness.

First, we as preachers must develop within ourselves "the courage to care." Eloquence and zeal become the hallmarks of our preaching when our hearts and our emotions are invested in the matter before us. . . .

[Second], the courage to care can quickly result in the courage to speak out on some issue. That means that we have to declare ourselves to be on one side or another of a certain issue or dispute. We are no longer neutral on the matter; we have pronounced to the world the words of Martin Luther before the Diet of Worms in the sixteenth century: "Here I stand!"

Then comes the third and final step on the road to prophetic ministry and prophetic preaching—namely, that once we have altered our own way of thinking about something and then changed our own lives appropriately we then set out to impact "our historical circumstances."

In prophetic ministry, and in prophetic preaching, the goal is not just to call attention to the matter at hand; the goal is to change our historical circumstances.[6]

While I deeply appreciate McMickle's reiteration of West's three-fold action agenda—and especially his call to keep in mind the goal of changing our historical circumstances (thus moving us beyond acts of charity to acts of advocacy)—I cannot help but notice that he skips fairly quickly over the need to change our own lives (assuming it has occurred in conjunction with our changed speaking). For some of us, however, the road from right thinking to right acting will not be navigated nearly so quickly. And perhaps this is a juncture at which some of the spiritual disciplines outlined in chapter 2 again become critical for prophetic witness.

If we are going to engage in prophetic acts, we will need to be in prayer, open to the Spirit's guidance as to which acts we are called to take on. If we are going to engage in prophetic acts, we will need to place ourselves intentionally in contexts where our hearts continue to be broken by the things that break the heart of God. If we are going to engage in prophetic acts, we will need wisdom and discernment regarding which actions might be most effective in bringing about the change to historical circumstances that West advocates. And if we are going to engage in prophetic acts, we will need to be surrounded by communities of faith and support who pray with and for us, who dance and rejoice with us when minor victories are won, and who, when we are despairing, speak to us of the hope that also lies at the heart of God's prophetic gospel.

A prophetic pastor friend once told me that it wasn't so much that he had picked the causes for which he became an advocate as that they had chosen him. "If you open yourself to the Spirit," he said, "you will find yourself in situations you never imagined where you are asked to speak and act on behalf of God's people." I think he is right. God's other name is "Surprise!" This is true not only in terms of how our lives often evolve but also in terms of the causes we may find ourselves advocating and the deeds we find ourselves doing for Jesus' sake.

But I also believe that what sustains prophetic actions (as well as prophetic speaking) over the long haul are the prayers and support of a community of like-minded people who band together and encourage one another in good times and bad. For some pastors, such a community will already exist within the congregation served. But other pastors will have to look outside the congregation to find a community with whom to share their visions, their joys, and their frustrations.

"Can prophetic actions sometimes take the place of prophetic sermons?" the pastor asked me that day. Of course, they can. The encouragement of St. Francis of Assisi that we preach the gospel—and use words only when necessary speaks truth at this juncture.

As a case in point, Richard Lischer reminds us of the power that certain symbolic actions had during the civil rights movement—actions that were altogether intentional on the part of the movement's prophetic leaders. He writes,

> Of course, it may appear that to interpret ordinary actions like walking or eating as prophetic signs of an imminent reality is to overinflate them with symbolic or theological significance. But how does one explain the irrational fear and anger that a sit-in or march engendered in white southerners? Outsiders have occasionally wondered why the authorities did not simply permit a group of Negroes to walk a few blocks to city hall without offering violent interference. What provoked these distorted grimaces and snarls on the faces of spectators, now frozen for history in old photographs and museum exhibits? Perhaps these Bible-believing southerners suspected what ancient Israel knew, that the actions of the prophets, just as surely as their words, are the signs of a new order that is rapidly approaching.
>
> Prophetic actions are harbingers of the future.[7]

Prophetic actions are indeed harbingers of the future, and as such they can sometimes stand alone. Yet it is also the case that at times prophetic actions need words to interpret or to inspire them. The two go hand in hand—much as Word and Sacrament do. So next we turn to a consideration of some of the options pastors might consider when integrating word and deed in the pulpit.

WORD AND DEED IN THE WITNESS OF THE SERMON
AND THE CONGREGATION

The Sermon as Reflection on Prophetic Action

One of the things that has intrigued me about the prophetic witness of William Sloane Coffin is the way in which he not only engaged in very public prophetic acts—accepting draft cards from Vietnam War resisters, blessing a shipment of wheat sent to North Vietnam in the aftermath of the Vietnam War, flying to Tehran to minister to American hostages held prisoner there—but the way he occasionally would use those actions as a basis for reflection in his Sunday morning sermons.

A prime example is found in the two sermons Coffin preached in December of 1979 when he and two other U.S. clergy persons were invited by the Iranian government to travel to Tehran to celebrate Christmas with American hostages held there. There was considerable controversy over the trip, for U.S. government officials had strongly discouraged it, and many Americans felt that the clergy were being used by the Iranians to bolster U.S. sympathy for their cause. But Coffin and the other clergy went anyhow, and the Sunday before his departure he preached a sermon titled "And Pray for the Iranians, Too."[8]

Coffin talked about his apprehension in going on the trip since "Americans are better talkers than listeners, especially when it comes to listening to people of countries smaller than our own."[9] "We scream about the hostages, but few Americans heard the scream of tortured Iranians."[10] He also spoke out strongly against engaging in the sanctions against Iran that the Carter administration was considering. ("I happen to believe that the present proposal to impose sanctions is highly reminiscent of Lyndon Johnson's bombing of North Vietnam; it will only put iron up the spine of the other side."[11]) And he called for a brand of patriotism that was "based on morality, and not defined by the needs of a militant unity," urging, "Rather than rally around the flag, let us gather around the Holy Child."[12]

Finally, he encouraged his parishioners to pray—and in doing so expanded the horizons of prayer:

> So, dear parishioners, pray for us. Pray for the hostages. And pray for the Iranians, too. Pray this Christmas that those who have offended may repent. Pray in this holy season, that the darkness of our impatience may not overcome the light of compassion; that the darkness

of growing violence may not quench the light of peace. Pray in the name of a child, the Prince of Peace.[13]

The following Sunday (the Sunday after his return from Iran), Coffin's sermon was titled "Report from Tehran."[14] He spent the sermon describing some of the key events of the trip: how he met with hostages in groups of four on Christmas Eve in rooms where they sang Christmas carols (with Coffin playing the piano); how they heard the Luke Christmas story read aloud; and how they all joined hands and prayed (including Iranian leaders and guards) that they might find a moment of grace in the midst of it all when "there would be neither captive nor captor, neither American nor Iranian."[15] He told about receiving the Christmas messages the hostages had written to their families in the United States, and about delivering a kiss to one of the captives from his small child who lived in Brooklyn. He insisted that both Iran and the United States had been wronged in the past, quoting answers he had received to some of the questions he had asked of the captors: "When I said to Mohammed that it was wrong to have hostages, his reply was, 'What's fifty-two days in captivity compared to twenty-six years under the Shah.'"[16] "When we asked why they were so angry at Carter as opposed to Kissinger and Nixon, who had upheld the Shah so much longer, they reminded us that Carter had said that he and the Shah saw eye to eye on human rights."[17] And Coffin once again urged Americans not to take a hard line against the Iranians by imposing sanctions, but instead to reciprocate their kindness in allowing the clergy access to the hostages by refusing to deport any more Iranian students studying in the United States.

This sermon, too, ended in a call to prayer. But once again, the definition of prayer was expanded:

> Prayer is an act of empathy, not an act of self-expression. Prayer is thinking God's thought after him—hard as that is. Prayer is really meaning, "Thy Will be done, not mine." Prayer is really meaning, "Thy Kingdom come, not mine." If both sides truly pray to the one God they both believe in, both sides will rise above their present condition.[18]

Ernest Campbell, "The Case for Reparations"[19]

Ernest Campbell, the senior minister who preceded Coffin at Riverside, also preached a significant sermon in which he reflected on a prophetic action. In Campbell's case, however, the prophetic action that provided the basis for reflection was not his own but that of another. On May 5, 1969, James Forman, spokesman for the Black Economic Development Conference, interrupted morning worship at The Riverside Church, insisting that the congregation, along with other Christian and Jewish communities, make reparations of $500 million to African Americans for their complicity in slavery and other economic injustices. The story made headline news around the nation and caused a great deal of controversy—not only locally but nationally and even internationally—as other denominational and religious bodies (including the National and World Councils of Churches) debated whether or not reparations were appropriate. Members of The Riverside Church were themselves divided over the issue—especially given the way in which Forman had made his demands and the fact that he wanted the reparations to go to his own organization that had as a stated goal the overthrow of the United States government. Some believed the incident should be ignored. Others felt drastic action should be taken against Forman, including opposition to his revolutionary rhetoric, and still others felt that some sort of response was required of Christians who believed in a God of justice.

Ernest Campbell did not preach on the matter immediately. Instead, he and the officers of Riverside Church entered into ongoing dialogue about Forman's demands. The church's board of deacons ultimately voted to establish a reparations fund (though the funds did not go to Forman's organization; they went to Manhattan-based organizations committed to economic development and social justice for minorities). In July—some ten weeks after the Forman incident—Campbell preached a sermon titled "The Case for Reparations."

The sermon began not with the issue at hand but with the biblical text for the day, the story of Zacchaeus (Luke 19:1–10). Campbell noted that there were two elements prominent in the reclamation of Zacchaeus—generosity and justice—and that after Jesus dined with him, Zacchaeus willingly chose to make reparations to those he had wronged. Campbell then drew an analogy between Zacchaeus's actions and the church's need to make reparations for the injustices meted out to African Americans at their hand. However, he also differentiated the church's aims from those of Forman, noting that the church should say yes to justice (in terms of making reparations) but no to the use of funds given to overthrow the U.S. government (as Forman had encouraged). The gospel, he insisted, pushes us to reparations for the sake of reconciliation.[20]

While most pastors I know will not have their worship interrupted by someone making demands for reparations or be invited by heads of governments to visit U.S. hostages held in captivity in a foreign land, we do have the opportunity to use the sermon as a starting place for reflection on prophetic actions—whether the action be our own or that of others. What if the pastor, whose face was frequently in the paper for his participation in antiwar demonstrations, used his sermon one Sunday to reflect on the reasons that he, as a Christian, participated in such acts and invited dialogue around his words and actions afterward? What if the pastor, whose college-student congregant had spent her spring break engaged in a protest at the School of the Americas in Americus, Georgia, and who had been arrested for her civil disobedience there, invited the parishioner to tell her story as a part of the Sunday sermon and then spent the rest of the sermon reflecting on the nature of Christian civil disobedience and its long history in the life of our nation and world? Or what if the preacher took a headline from the local newspaper about demonstrations at a local factory over fair pay and better health-care benefits for workers, and used it as a window into the life of the working poor and the challenges they face in surviving financially?

Using the sermon as an opportunity to reflect on the biblical and ethical implications of prophetic actions is a highly provocative way to move the sermon focus from the issue itself to theological reflection on it. In another context I have argued that parish preachers are actually "local theologians" who bring the Bible and theology and life experiences together in an integrative, fitting, and transformative way for a particular people in a particular time and place.[21] In the process pastors are not only crafting theology for their parishioners; they are also modeling for them how to become local theologians themselves. Prophetic actions often pose a prime opportunity for such reflection and modeling to take place in the pulpit and beyond.

The Sermon as a Call to Prophetic Action

If we truly believe that it is the *church* that is called to give prophetic witness and not just the pastor, then sermons on prophetic issues will necessarily call on the entire Christian community to become involved in actions on behalf of God's justice in the world. Many pastors know this and end their prophetic sermons with some call to action. However, often the challenges for the pastor are (1) which action(s) to propose, and 2) how to facilitate such actions after the service is over.

In terms of which actions to propose, knowledge of the congregational context becomes critical, for action that is most fitting in one context may differ significantly from that which is fitting and appropriate in another.[22] In *Preaching Justice,* Christine Smith demonstrates that justice issues vary greatly given the social location of the congregation.[23] The eight authors of the volume, chosen from diverse ethnic and cultural communities, write about justice from their own vantage points, and it becomes readily apparent that while there may be common themes in some of the issues faced by Native American, African American, Latino, and Asian American congregations in the United States (such as their common experiences of racial prejudice and discrimination), there are also significant differences among them. The legal issues facing the Lakota tribe of South Dakota (related to nonobservance of treaties made with Native Americans by the U.S. government) are different from the crises of assimilation faced by first- and second-generation Korean American immigrants to the United States. In a similar vein, it may well be the case that rural farm workers will face different justice issues than urban office workers, and that congregations comprised of minority populations will face different issues than those comprised of majority populations. Not only do such differences affect how and what we preach prophetically; they also affect the naming of actions that are appropriate and fitting for particular contexts. The actions appropriate for a fifty-member small-town congregation comprised primarily of retirees on fixed incomes may differ significantly from the actions proposed for an affluent congregation of twelve hundred in the suburbs of a large city.

A second consideration for the pastor is whether to offer multiple options for action or only one option. The advantage of multiple options is that they allow congregants to express themselves in a diversity of ways that may fit their varied readiness factors. For example, while some congregants may be at a stage of conviction at which they are willing to engage in civil disobedience or join a protest march, others may be more comfortable signing petitions, writing letters to their congressional representatives, or simply attending a forum class that allows them to continue developing their point of view. All may be valid avenues for action—depending on the stage and depth of commitment on the part of the actor.

On the other hand, sometimes offering a single option for participation focuses response to the issue and allows congregants not only a united way to make a stand but also one concrete thing they can do in the midst of their already-busy lives. Several years ago a student at Yale Divinity School preached a compelling sermon on immigration reform during our daily chapel service. She ended her sermon not by calling for multiple actions but by challenging our community to unite in undertaking one very concrete local action. At the time, the city of New Haven had become one of the first cities in the nation to allow undocumented immigrants to secure a residence card that provided them with a means of legal identification. One of the concerns, however, was that if only undocumented people possessed these identification cards, it would be easy for businesses to target them and to refuse them the services desired. This student ended her sermon in chapel by asking all of us—students, faculty, and staff—to go down to the place in the city where the cards were to be issued the following week and to apply for a residence card so that proprietors of local business could not tell undocumented immigrants from other community citizens. Many in our community responded positively to her call, welcoming the opportunity to have one simple thing they could do to foster greater justice in our community.

Third, as much as possible, it is important to lift up and celebrate the prophetic actions that are already taking place within a congregation and to place a new call to action within the framework of what is already happening. If there is a group within the church that will be traveling to Washington, DC, to take part in a peace demonstration, lift up and celebrate that act within worship—inviting others to participate either by marching with them or by signing letters to Congress members after the service. If there is a group within the congregation that is deeply committed to environmental concerns, reinforce their call to the congregation to engage in a "greening" during the Lenten season as a spiritual discipline. If there is a group within the church who do volunteer tutoring with inner-city schoolchildren, invite them to tell some of their stories as part of a sermon that focuses on the systemic issues related to education and poverty. Churches, like individuals, often grow best when they are affirmed and celebrated for what they are already doing. And nearly every church has people within it who are engaged in small but significant acts of prophetic witness in their communities, places of work, or volunteer organizations.

Finally, it is important to note that sometimes sermons that call for prophetic action need significant advance preparation and coordination with other bodies within the congregation before they are preached. Ernest Campbell's sermon on reparations is a case in point, since by the time he preached it, the board of deacons of Riverside Church had already adopted a plan of action that Campbell was also endorsing from the pulpit. Even when preaching on less volatile issues, however, some advance preparation can be helpful. For when people become inspired by prophetic preaching and are ready to engage in actions on behalf of justice, it is important to have some vehicles for action readily available for them.

In a course I taught on prophetic preaching at Yale Divinity School, students were divided into teams of four to preach on specific social issues (war, poverty, racism, ecology, and human sexuality). A part of their assignment was to brainstorm together and to come up with a list of ways that congregations might be invited to respond to their sermons. I was impressed not only with their creativity in taking on this task but also with the wide diversity of possible responses they envisioned—which ran the gamut from praying about an issue, to firsthand involvement in relief efforts, to actions designed to affect systemic change. Below I include a partial list of suggested actions put forward by a student team that worked on global poverty and economic justice.[24] While their suggestions are specifically related to that particular topic, this listing could easily serve as a template for pastors and laity in brainstorming about possible actions related to other social justice issues.

— Hold a "One Book/One Congregation" event, challenging everyone in the parish to read the same book about issues related to global poverty, and then host an evening of book discussion, including dinner and facilitated small groups.

— Create a special Communion service that intertwines the themes of "Eucharist" and "Hunger." Hold a special collection to be given to the local food bank.

— Hold a parish-wide bake sale/auction: ask parishioners (including kids) to bake their most fantastic creations. Then auction off the pies and cakes for $50 to $300 and sell cookies for small amounts so that all can participate. Use the proceeds for an organization that addresses global poverty (such as Heifer International).

— Create a group to go on a "reverse mission" trip to a part of the world that lives in poverty; live with a Christian community there and at the same level as the average person would in that country. Use this time to learn about the faith and living conditions of others around the world.

—Create a speakers series to follow up your sermon. Invite speakers from organizations that work on poverty issues to talk to your church and to help the church choose a concrete way that it can work for justice to combat the structural causes of poverty.

—Get involved in microfinancing, either through an established organization such as Opportunity International, Kiva, or Grameen Foundation, or by creating a microfinancing organization of your own directly with a community with which your church is already involved.

—Bring in trainers from an organization like Results (www.results.org) to help parishioners become savvy about lobbying political leaders on issues related to poverty. Encourage parishioners to organize lobbying parties in their homes.

Worship and Preaching as Prophetic Actions

Finally, lest we draw too fine a line between word and deed in Christian witness it is important to acknowledge that whenever Christians gather in Jesus' name to proclaim that the crucified One is our sovereign and that we owe our ultimate allegiance and devotion to God alone, we are already engaging in highly subversive and prophetic activity. While we tend to domesticate worship and sometimes fail to realize its prophetic potential, worship itself at best is a highly countercultural act. For as we gather around Word and Table to give worship and praise to the crucified Lamb, we are also declaring to the world by our actions *and* our words that our God reigns supreme, that all other pretenders to the throne are bogus, and that one day the earth will be as full of the glory and justice and righteousness of God as the waters that cover the sea. One day God's reign will fully be known on earth, even as it is known in heaven.

New Testament scholar Brian Blount reminds us that Jesus' own prophetic preaching was part and parcel of his prophetic ministry and it is difficult to draw a distinction between word and deed in his ministry.

In his person [Jesus] represents God's divine intervention. He compels people to leave their pasts and follow him. He speaks authoritatively with demons. He teaches with supernatural authority. He exorcises and heals. But these are not the ways he represents the kingdom. *They are manifestations of his preaching.* The preaching is the way Jesus intervenes. Preaching, in Mark's narration, is what shatters the boundaries. It is the form of God's intervention.[25]

Blount argues that the original ending of Mark's Gospel—in which the women run from the empty tomb and say nothing to anyone because they are afraid—is intentional, since the author of Mark's Gospel believes it is up to the church to complete the story. This Gospel calls the church, like Jesus, to "Go, preach!"—to preach the boundary-breaking news of God's reign in their midst, even though it may lead to persecution and even death.[26]

In his book *The Word before the Powers*, Charles Campbell also envisions the preaching ministry of Jesus as being a significant part of his prophetic activity. Jesus, says Campbell, came preaching peace. By so doing he engaged the principalities and powers of his day, yet in a way that avoided both passivity and violence. Instead, Jesus engaged in nonviolent resistance.

> Jesus does not become the evil he opposes. He does not take the path of violence. Rather, he limits himself to the "sword of the Spirit."
> . . . Jesus sticks to preaching for that is the means that is ethically consistent with the peaceable reign of God he inaugurates. Through his preaching, Jesus engages in a "third way" that avoids both passivity and violence. . . . And it is this third way that overcomes the powers, breaks their ultimate ability to enslave us and creates a space for resistance and newness.[27]

In like manner, says Campbell, preachers today are called to reenact Jesus' way of nonviolent resistance through their own proclamation. Refusing to follow the ways of domination, coercion, or violence, preachers follow "the way of risky, nonviolent engagement with the powers."[28]

> In moral obedience, shaped by the pattern established by Jesus, the preaching of the church takes the path of nonviolent resistance, rather than coercion or domination, in the face of those who oppose God's reign. Apart from all words spoken, the practice of preaching itself proclaims that the church does not resort to violence in the name of truth; rather it witnesses. . . . Indeed, in the act of witnessing to Jesus, the church reminds itself that a resort to violence is a

contradiction of the one whom we preach and the beloved community we seek.[29]

PREACHING THE FUTURE OF GOD

Campbell and Blount rightly remind us that preaching itself can be a highly prophetic act of confrontation with the principalities and powers of this world. However, if we are going to reclaim it as such, we will also need to recover the eschatological theology that lies at the heart of all prophetic witness. We witness to the coming peaceable and boundary-breaking reign of God because we believe that God's reign has already broken into our midst in the person of Jesus of Nazareth, and that God will one day bring it to completion. Our ultimate hope rests not in ourselves but in God. Yet God also uses us here and now to bring that future reality into the present day.

Liturgical scholar Don Saliers notes that one of the distinguishing characteristics of twentieth-century theology was its reorientation of how Christians think about eschatology:

> Whereas traditionally the term has been used to refer to the "doctrine of last things"—final judgment, death, heaven and hell—it has, in contemporary theology, come to be a principle of thought. That is, to posit any Christian claim about God and the world requires considering it *from the standpoint of the future of God.*[30]

Preaching, however, sometimes still functions on the basis of older notions of eschatology rather than considering the present from the standpoint of the future of God. Indeed, Tom Long mourns the fact that the church today seems to have lost its true eschatological voice and has substituted for it either a conservative literalism (as in the Left Behind book series) or a liberal progressivism that trusts too much in human effort. Long calls preachers back to an eschatology that is grounded in hope in God's already-present yet also-coming reign:

> To preach eschatologically is to participate in the promise that the fullness of God's *shalom* flows into the present, drawing it toward consummation. Eschatological preaching brings the finished work of God to bear on an unfinished world, summoning it to completion. Progress preaching tells people to gird up their loins and to use the resources at hand to make the world into a better place, and such preaching necessarily condemns people to failure and despair.

Eschatological preaching promises a "new heaven and a new earth" and invites people to participate in a coming future that, while it is not dependent upon their success, is open to the labors of their hands.[31]

If worship and preaching are going to reclaim their cutting prophetic edge, it will be important that they also regain an eschatological focus. For it is our belief in God's promised future that gives us hope and courage to persevere in the present. As Long puts it, "Preaching eschatologically today means helping our people know that the eschatological and apocalyptic language of the Bible is not about predicting the future; it is primarily a way of seeing the present in the light of hope."[32]

PROPHETS: HARBINGERS OF HOPE

At the outset of this book, I said that I have been drawn to the witness of the prophets in my lifetime because ultimately they offer hope: hope of a new day to come when justice will roll down like waters, and righteousness, like an ever-flowing stream (Amos 5:24). Somehow, then, it seems highly appropriate that at this book's conclusion I should come back full circle to hope.

This world of ours desperately needs hope, and prophets are uniquely equipped by God to bring it. In the midst of the lies and half-truths and doublespeak that are prevalent in our culture, prophets speak truth. In the midst of willful ignorance or avoidance of the injustices that surround us, prophets compel us to see and to respond to the evils of our day. And in the midst of the bleak realities of war and discrimination and poverty and patriotism gone awry—the way things are—prophets invite us to envision and to live into what will be: the future as God intends it.

Mary Catherine Hilkert rightly locates the ultimate hope for Christian preaching in the promise of Jesus' resurrection:

If the resurrection is possible, then all of reality holds a possibility beyond human control or imagination—God's possibility.

The preacher is called to narrate the community's familiar story, but from a new vantage point—from the perspective of the new and different future that God has promised and that the resurrection has inaugurated. In remembering God's surprising but steadfast faithfulness in the past, the community hears the promise spoken again in their midst and has the courage to "hope against hope" that God can and will be faithful in this new moment and in the unknown future that lies ahead.[33]

Christian prophets invite their communities to "hope against hope" that God's new future is already impinging on present realities. To become such a prophet will require a radical commitment to what Brad Braxton calls "righteous troublemaking . . . the agitation that results from speaking the truth in love—the truth, the whole truth, and nothing but the truth."[34] Such troublemaking today—as in biblical times—stems not from a lack of love for our people but from an abundance of love for them, for God, and for our world. For only those who love deeply can also speak truth from a deep place of passion and compassion.

To become such a prophet will also require courage—the kind that grows out of a deep-rooted and faith-filled spirituality, for prophetic preaching can be costly. Martin Luther King Jr. frequently likened his own persecution and imprisonment to that of the apostle Paul and also identified strongly with the suffering and death of Jesus.[35] But King, like other prophets before him—including the prophet Jesus—also saw redemptive possibilities even in his suffering.

Perhaps, at its heart, prophetic witness both attracts and repels preachers because it cuts so close to the heart of the gospel, with its call to follow Jesus in the way of suffering love. We cannot do it in our own strength. But in the strength of the God who empowered prophets from Amos and Jeremiah and Micah to Jesus and Sojourner Truth and King, and who always offers us resurrection possibilities, all things are possible.

Permissions

Notes

Introduction

1. Henry W. Longfellow, "I Heard the Bells on Christmas Day," in *The International Book of Christmas Carols*, ed. Walter Ehret and George K. Evans (Brattleboro, VT: Stephen Greene Press, 1980), 58. The language for God has been changed by the author to make it more inclusive.

2. Walter Brueggemann, *The Prophetic Imagination* (Philadelphia: Fortress Press, 1978), 13.

3. Ibid., 60.

4. The book is titled *The History of the Riverside Church in the City of New York* (New York: New York University Press, 2004). Authors include Peter J. Paris, John W. Cook, James Hudnut-Beumler, Lawrence H. Mamiya, Leonora Tubbs Tisdale, and Judith Weisenfeld.

5. In an interview the team of authors conducted with James Forbes, Forbes said that what he felt Riverside Church needed when he came as pastor was a "spirituality for activism." The church was strong in its prophetic witness and activism, but it needed a spirituality that would undergird, support, and inform it. See Paris et al., *History of the Riverside Church*, 111–15.

6. The possible exception is Fifth Avenue Presbyterian Church in New York, which, while predominantly white and middle to upper class, also has members representing over forty different nationalities, as well as poor and homeless members.

Chapter 1: Where Have All the Prophets Gone?

1. Garrison Keillor, "Prophet," on *Lake Wobegon U.S.A.: Fertility*, audio CD (Highbridge Audio: 1993).

2. Marvin A. McMickle, *Where Have All the Prophets Gone? Reclaiming Prophetic Preaching in America* (Cleveland: Pilgrim Press, 2006).

3. Ibid., 119–20.

4. Ibid., 120.

5. Ibid., 119–42.

6. J. Philip Wogaman, *Speaking the Truth in Love: Prophetic Preaching to a Broken World* (Louisville, KY: Westminster John Knox Press, 1998), 3.

7. Ibid.

8. Ibid., 4. The poem "Columbus" is taken from James Russell Lowell, *The Poetical Works of James Russell Lowell* (Boston: James R. Osgood & Co., 1876), 59.

9. Ibid.

10. Dawn Ottoni-Wilhelm, "God's Word in the World: Prophetic Preaching and the Gospel of Jesus Christ," in *Anabaptist Preaching: A Conversation Between Pulpit, Pew & Bible*, ed. David B. Greiser and Michael A. King (Telford, PA: Cascadia Publishing House, 2003), 77.

11. Ibid., 84–91.

12. Kelly Miller Smith, *Social Crisis Preaching: The Lyman Beecher Lectures 1983* (Macon, GA: Mercer University Press, 1984).

13. Justo L. and Catherine González, *Liberation Preaching: The Pulpit and the Oppressed*, ed. William D. Thompson (Nashville: Abingdon Press, 1980).

14. Christine Marie Smith, ed., *Preaching Justice: Ethnic and Cultural Perspectives* (Cleveland: United Church Press, 1998).

15. Walter Brueggemann, *The Prophetic Imagination* (Philadelphia: Fortress Press, 1978), 13.

16. Ibid. Italics added for emphasis.

17. McMickle, *Where Have All the Prophets Gone?*, 11. Quotation is from Brueggemann, *Prophetic Imagination*, 44.

18. Ibid., 19. Quotations are from Abraham Joshua Heschel, *The Prophets* (New York: Harper & Row, 1962), 224–25.

19. John McClure, *Preaching Words: 144 Key Terms in Homiletics* (Louisville, KY: Westminster John Knox Press, 2007), 117.

20. Cornel West, *Democracy Matters: Winning the Fight Against Imperialism* (New York: Penguin Press, 2004), 114.

21. Ibid., 114–15.

22. See Brian K. Blount, *Go Preach! Mark's Kingdom Message and the Black Church Today* (Maryknoll, NY: Orbis Press, 1998). For examples of how Blount and coauthor Gary Charles bring this prophetic gospel to bear in their sermons, preached in very different contexts, see their volume *Preaching Mark in Two Voices* (Louisville, KY: Westminster John Knox Press, 2002).

23. Brueggemann, *Prophetic Imagination*, 20.

24. Ibid., 21.

25. Carol Lakey Hess, *Caretakers of Our Common House: Women's Development in Communities of Faith* (Nashville: Abingdon Press, 1997), 182.

26. Ibid., 184. Here Hess is building on the work of Mary Field Belenky et al., *Women's Ways of Knowing: The Development of Self, Voice, and Mind* (New York: Baker Books, 1986), and the distinctions the authors observe between women who are "constructed" knowers and those who are "separate" knowers.

27. Ibid., 185.

28. For more information on the work of this task force, go to www.pcusa.org/peaceunitypurity/.

29. Barbara K. Lundblad, *Transforming the Stone: Preaching Through Resistance to Change* (Nashville: Abingdon Press, 2001), 14–18.

30. Scott Bader-Saye, *Following Jesus in a Culture of Fear* (Grand Rapids: Brazos Press, 2007), 67.

31. Ibid., 68.

32. James M. Childs Jr., "Enabling Grace," in *Just Preaching: Prophetic Voices for Economic Justice*, ed. André Resner Jr. (St. Louis: Chalice Press, 2003), 40.

Chapter 2: Rekindling the Fire Within

1. Walter J. Burghardt, SJ, *Preaching the Just Word* (New Haven, CT: Yale University Press, 1996), ix.

2. Joan Chittister, *There Is a Season* (Maryknoll, NY: Orbis Books, 1996), 109.

3. James A. Forbes Jr. talked about the concept of a "spirituality for activism" on June 11, 2000, in an interview with a team of scholars who were writing *The History of the Riverside Church in the City of New York* (see note 5, introduction). He said that when he first came to be senior pastor of Riverside Church, the church was strong on activism but sometimes lacked a spiritual underpinning for its witness in the world. Forbes, coming from a Pentecostal tradition, felt that one of the things he could offer the church was a "spirituality for activism."

4. Chittister, *There Is a Season*, 109.

5. Ibid.

6. Leonora Tubbs Tisdale, "The Legacy of Riverside's Free Pulpit," in *The History of the Riverside Church in the City of New York*, Peter Paris et al. (New York: New York University Press, 2004), 76. These words from Fosdick's charge to McCracken were quoted in the *New York Herald Tribune*, October 3, 1946.

7. See Loren Pope, *Colleges That Change Lives: 40 Schools That Will Change the Way You Think about Colleges* (New York: Penguin Press, 2006).

8. Rick Ufford-Chase, "Reflections from the Moderator," a sermon preached at Fifth Avenue Presbyterian Church, New York City, December 4, 2005.

9. Ibid. These words of Gustavo Gutiérrez were paraphrased by Ufford-Chase (via Robert McAfee Brown).

10. Dieter T. Hessel, *Social Ministry*, rev. ed. (Louisville, KY: Westminster/John Knox Press, 1992), 97.

11. Ibid., 100.

12. Ibid., 100–101.

13. J. Randall Nichols, *The Restoring Word: Preaching as Pastoral Communication* (San Francisco: Harper & Row, 1987), 59.

14. Ibid., 60.

15. Ibid., 64.

16. See Harry Emerson Fosdick, "The Unknown Soldier," in *The Riverside Preachers*, ed. Paul Sherry (New York: Pilgrim Press, 1978), 49–58.

17. Some of the material in this section on Fosdick is also discussed in Tisdale, "Legacy of Riverside's Free Pulpit," 72–73.

18. Barbara K. Lundblad, *Transforming the Stone: Preaching Through Resistance to Change* (Nashville: Abingdon Press, 2001), 15.

19. Ibid.

20. Ibid., 16–17.

21. Scott Bader-Saye, *Following Jesus in a Culture of Fear* (Grand Rapids: Brazos Press, 2007), 69.

22. Ibid. Bader-Saye gives credit for the term "maintenance churches" to Claude Payne and Hamilton Beazley, *Reclaiming the Great Commission* (New York: Jossey-Bass, 2000).

23. Ibid., 71.

24. Some of the material that follows is paraphrased from Tisdale, "Legacy of Riverside's Free Pulpit," 55–135.

25. Ernest T. Campbell, "An Open Letter to Billy Graham," in Sherry, *Riverside Preachers*, 127.

26. Tisdale, "Legacy of Riverside's Free Pulpit," 99.

27. Interview with James A. Forbes Jr. by the Riverside Church History Project authors, June 10, 2000.

Chapter 3: Speaking Truth in Love

1. Martin Luther King Jr., "Loving Your Enemies," in *Strength to Love* (Philadelphia: Fortress Press, 1981), 54.

2. See Paul Tillich, *Theology of Culture*, ed. Robert C. Kimball (New York: Oxford University Press, 1959). I also discuss this distinction in Leonora Tubbs Tisdale, *Preaching as Local Theology and Folk Art* (Minneapolis: Fortress Press, 1997), 34–35.

3. J. Philip Wogaman, *Speaking Truth in Love: Prophetic Preaching to a Broken World* (Louisville, KY: Westminster John Knox Press, 1998), 19.

4. Ibid., 20–21.

5. Barbara K. Lundblad, *Transforming the Stone: Preaching Through Resistance to Change* (Nashville: Abingdon Press, 2001), 53–55.

6. Tex Sample, *U.S. Lifestyles and Mainline Churches* (Louisville, KY: Westminster/John Knox Press, 1990), 74–75.

7. Ibid. I also tell this story in Tisdale, *Preaching as Local Theology*, 115–16.

8. James A. Forbes Jr., a paraphrase from a videotaped sermon, as quoted in Lundblad, *Transforming the Stone*, 53–54.

9. Holly Haile Davis, "Three Moons in My Moccasins," in *Those Preaching Women: A Multicultural Collection*, ed. Ella Pearson Mitchell and Valerie Bridgeman Davis (Valley Forge, PA: Judson Press, 2008), 115–20. This sermon was preached on March 28, 2007, at the Bridgehampton Presbyterian Church for

the Long Island Presbytery meeting, where a Tabutne' meal in the Indian tradition was celebrated. The biblical text on which the sermon was based was John 12:20–33.

10. Ibid., 118.

11. Ibid., 119.

12. Barbara K. Lundblad, "An Easy Chair at the Laundromat," in Lundblad, *Transforming the Stone*, 113–19.

13. Ibid., 113.

14. Ibid., 118.

15. Emilie Townes, "The Valley before the Vision," a sermon preached in Marquand Chapel at Yale Divinity School on "Coming Out Day," October 7, 2005. Used by permission of the author. Townes is Associate Dean of Academic Affairs and Professor of African American Religion and Theology at Yale Divinity School.

16. Walter Brueggemann, "The Preacher, the Text and the People," *Theology Today* 47 (October 1990): 237–47. Brueggemann adopts the concept of "triangling" from family therapists Murray Bowen, *Family Therapy in Clinical Practice* (New York: J. Aranson, 1978); and Edwin H. Friedman, *Generation to Generation: Family Process in Church and Synagogue* (New York: Guilford Press, 1985). See also my discussion in Tisdale, *Preaching as Local Theology*, 50–51.

17. David Bartlett, "Woe to Us," *Journal for Preachers* 31, no. 2 (Lent 2008): 33–34. The sermon was preached at Columbia Theological Seminary, Decatur, Georgia, and was based on Jeremiah 17:5–10 and Luke 6:17–26.

18. Brian K. Blount, "Stay Close," in *Preaching Mark in Two Voices*, by Brian K. Blount and Gary W. Charles (Louisville, KY: Westminster John Knox Press, 2002), 170–80. Blount, who was on the faculty of Princeton Theological Seminary when he first preached this sermon, is currently president of Union Theological Seminary in Richmond, Virginia.

19. Ibid., 179–80.

20. Timothy Hart-Andersen, "The Prophetic Voice of the Church," a sermon preached at Westminster Presbyterian Church in Minneapolis, Minnesota, January 28, 2007. Used by permission of the author. The Scripture texts on which the sermon was based are Jeremiah 1:4–10 and Luke 4:21–30.

21. Ibid.

22. William Sloane Coffin Jr., "Warring Madness," in *The Riverside Preachers*, ed. Paul H. Sherry (New York: Pilgrim Press, 1978), 154–59.

23. Ibid., 159.

24. James A. Forbes Jr., "Emancipation from Poverty," in *Just Preaching: Prophetic Voices for Social Justice*, ed. André Resner Jr. (St. Louis: Chalice Press, 2003), 111–18.

25. Ibid., 113.

26. Ibid., 113–14.

27. Susan Murtha and Sharon Cody, "Finding the Right Well," a sermon preached at First Congregational Church, Guilford, Connecticut, February 24, 2008. Used by permission of the author.

28. William Sloane Coffin and Jim Johnson, "AIDS," in *The Collected Sermons of William Sloane Coffin: The Riverside Years,* Vol. 2 (Louisville, KY: Westminster John Knox Press, 2008), 353–58. This sermon was preached at The Riverside Church in New York City, January 28, 1986.

29. Ibid., 357–58.

30. Ibid., 358.

31. Nancy Duff credits her PhD adviser, Christopher L. Morse, Dietrich Bonhoeffer Professor of Theology and Ethics at Union Theological Seminary in New York City, for first teaching her this debate strategy.

32. William J. Carl III, *Preaching Christian Doctrine* (Philadelphia: Fortress Press, 1984), 122.

33. Charles Campbell, *The Word on the Street: Performing the Scriptures in the Urban Context* (Grand Rapids: Wm. B. Eerdmans Publishing Co., 2000), 77. The quotations are from Walter Wink, "Neither Passivity Nor Violence: Jesus' Third Way," *Forum* 7 (March/June 1992): 12.

34. Ibid., 77.

35. Desmond Tutu's remarks are quoted by Allan Boesak in his sermon "The LORD and the lords," in *Walking on Thorns: The Call to Christian Obedience* (Geneva: World Council of Churches, 1984), 10.

36. Lundblad, *Transforming the Stone,* 121.

Chapter 4: Giving Shape to the Witness

1. Thomas G. Long, *The Witness of Preaching,* 2nd ed. (Louisville, KY: Westminster John Knox Press, 2005), 118.

2. Long refers to what preachers want a sermon to say as its "focus" and what they hope it will do in the lives of their hearers as its "function." See ibid., 99–116.

3. Scott Black Johnston, "Blessing and Cursing," a sermon preached at Trinity Presbyterian Church in Atlanta, Georgia, July 17, 2005. Used by permission of the author. The sermon was the fourth in a series focused on "God and Human Relationships." Black Johnston is currently pastor of Fifth Avenue Presbyterian Church in New York City.

4. Whitney Rice, "The Blood That Cries Out from the Ground." This sermon was first preached in Nouwen Chapel at Yale Divinity School in May 2008 as a part of a class titled "Prophetic Preaching." Used by permission of the author. Rice is an Episcopal curate at Christ Church Cathedral in Indianapolis, Indiana.

5. Edmund A. Steimle, Morris J. Niedenthal, and Charles L. Rice, *Preaching the Story* (Philadelphia: Fortress Press, 1980).

6. Barbara K. Lundblad, "No Small Thing," in *Transforming the Stone: Preaching Through Resistance to Change* (Nashville: Abingdon Press, 2001), 133–38. Lundblad is professor of homiletics at Union Theological Seminary in New York.

7. Ibid., 133.

8. Ibid., 135.

9. Ibid., 136.

10. Ibid., 137.

11. Ibid., 138.

12. Ronald J. Allen, *Patterns of Preaching: A Sermon Sampler* (St. Louis: Chalice Press, 1998), 36.

13. Martin Luther King Jr. "How Should a Christian View Communism?" in *Strength to Love* (Philadelphia: Fortress Press, 1981), 97–106.

14. Ibid., 97.

15. Ibid.

16. Ibid., 98.

17. Ibid.

18. Ibid., 99.

19. Ibid., 100.

20. Ibid.

21. Ibid., 100–102.

22. Ibid., 103.

23. Ibid., 104.

24. Ibid., 105.

25. Sheila Nelson-McJilton, "Crumbs," in *Preaching as Prophetic Calling: Sermons That Work XII*, ed. Roger Alling and David Schlafer (Harrisburg, PA: Morehouse Publishing, 2004), 100–103. Nelson-McJilton was associate rector of Christ Church, Stevensville, Maryland, when she preached this sermon at the Episcopal Preaching Foundation's annual "Preaching Excellence Conference."

26. Ibid., 102.

27. Ibid., 102–3.

28. Ibid., 103.

29. Veronica Goines, "Neckbone Faith," in *More Power in the Pulpit: How America's Most Effective Black Preachers Prepare Their Sermons*, ed. Cleophus J. LaRue (Louisville, KY: Westminster John Knox Press, 2009), 52–57. Goines is pastor of the historic and multicultural St. Andrew Presbyterian Church in Marin City, California.

30. Ibid., 54.

31. Ibid.

32. Ibid., 55.

33. Ibid., 57.

34. Ibid.

35. Ibid.

36. Martin Luther King Jr., "Paul's Letter to American Christians, Sermon Delivered to the Commission on Ecumenical Mission and Relations, United Presbyterian Church U.S.A.," in *The Papers of Martin Luther King, Jr.,* vol. 6: *Advocate of the Social Gospel, September 1948–March 1963,* ed. Clayborne Carson (Berkeley: University of California Press, 2007), 338–46. This sermon was preached on June 3, 1958, in Pittsburgh, PA.

37. Ibid., 339–40.

38. Ibid.

39. Ibid., 340.

40. Ibid., 340–45.

41. Ibid., 340–41.

42. Ibid., 345.

43. Ibid., 345–46.

44. Ibid., 346.

45. Ernest T. Campbell, "An Open Letter to Billy Graham," in *The Riverside Preachers,* ed. Paul H. Sherry (New York: Pilgrim Press, 1978), 125–31. This sermon was first preached at The Riverside Church in New York City on December 31, 1972.

46. Ibid., 125.

47. Ibid.

48. Ibid., 126.

49. Ibid., 127–28.

50. Ibid., 129.

51. Ibid., 129–30.

52. Ibid., 131.

53. Walter Burghardt, SJ, "God's Justice and America's Sixth Child" in *Just Preaching: Prophetic Voices for Economic Justice,* ed. André Resner Jr. (St. Louis: Chalice Press, 2003), 131–36. Burghardt, now deceased, was a Jesuit priest who was widely known for his deep commitment to prophetic and socially relevant preaching.

54. Ibid., 131–33.

55. Ibid., 134.

56. Ibid., 135.

57. Ronald J. Allen, "Come, Sophia," in *The Teaching Sermon* (Nashville: Abingdon Press, 1995), 105–9. Allen is professor of homiletics at Christian Theological Seminary in Indianapolis, Indiana.

58. Ibid., 107.

59. Ibid., 109.

60. Ibid.

61. Leonora Tubbs Tisdale, "Beautiful Feet and Labor Pains," a sermon preached at Union Theological Seminary in Richmond, Virginia, February 2, 1988.

62. Teresa Fry Brown, "Justice or Just Us?" a sermon preached at Trinity Presbyterian Church in Atlanta, November 2, 2007, as part of the national conference

of the Covenant Network of Presbyterians. Used by permission of the author. Fry Brown is associate professor of homiletics at Candler School of Theology and an ordained minister in the African Methodist Episcopal Church.

63. See Eugene Lowry, *The Homiletical Plot*, exp. ed. (Louisville, KY: Westminster John Knox Press, 2000).

64. Brian K. Blount, "God on the Loose," in *Preaching Mark in Two Voices*, by Brian K. Blount and Gary W. Charles (Louisville, KY: Westminster John Knox Press, 2002), 28–36.

65. Ibid., 29.

66. Ibid.

67. Ibid., 31.

68. Ibid., 32.

69. Ibid., 34.

70. Ibid., 35.

71. Carolyn Sharp, "Refuse to Be Consoled," a sermon preached in Marquand Chapel at Yale Divinity School, September 8, 2005. Used by permission of the author. Sharp is a professor of Hebrew Scriptures at the Divinity School.

72. Susan Durber, "The Massacre of the Innocents," in *Silence in Heaven: A Book of Women's Preaching*, ed. Susan Durber and Heather Walton (London: SCM Press, 1994), 110–15. This sermon was first preached on the First Sunday of Epiphany 1992 and was based on Matthew 2:1–18.

73. Ibid., 111.

74. Ibid., 114.

75. Ibid., 114–15.

76. Ibid., 115.

77. Ibid.

78. Harry Emerson Fosdick, "The Unknown Soldier," in Sherry, *The Riverside Preachers*, 49–58. This sermon was first preached at The Riverside Church in New York City on Armistice Day, November 12, 1933.

79. Ibid., 49–50.

80. Ibid., 50.

81. Ibid.

82. Ibid., 57–58.

Chapter 5: Word *and* Deed

1. Cornel West, *Democracy Matters: Winning the Fight Against Imperialism* (New York: Penguin Press, 2004), 172.

2. Marvin A. McMickle, "Prophetic Preaching in the 21st Century: It Is Not Just About the Words," *The African American Pulpit* 11, no. 4 (Fall 2008): 17.

3. Ibid.

4. Allan Boesak, "Prophetic Faithfulness," in *Best Sermons* 3, ed. James Cox (San Francisco: Harper Collins, 1990), 149–56. This sermon was preached in

Louisville, KY, at the dedication of the national headquarters of the Presbyterian Church (U.S.A.).

5. Ibid., 154.

6. Cornel West as paraphrased in McMickle, "Prophetic Preaching," 17–18.

7. Richard Lischer, *The Preacher King: Martin Luther King, Jr., and the Word That Moved America* (New York: Oxford University Press, 1995), 183.

8. William Sloane Coffin, "And Pray for the Iranians, Too," in *The Collected Sermons of William Sloane Coffin: The Riverside Years*, vol. 1 (Louisville, KY: Westminster John Knox Press, 2008), 270–72. This sermon was preached at The Riverside Church in New York City on December 23, 1979.

9. Ibid., 270.

10. Ibid., 271.

11. Ibid., 272.

12. Ibid.

13. Ibid.

14. William Sloane Coffin, "Report from Tehran," in *Collected Sermons*, 1: 272–79. This sermon was preached at The Riverside Church in New York City on December 30, 1979.

15. Ibid., 275.

16. Ibid., 277.

17. Ibid.

18. Ibid., 279.

19. Ernest T. Campbell, "The Case for Reparations," *The Riverside Preachers*, ed. Paul H. Sherry (New York: Pilgrim Press, 1978), 118–24. This sermon was preached at The Riverside Church in New York City on July 13, 1969.

20. Ibid., 123–24.

21. See Leonora Tubbs Tisdale, *Preaching as Local Theology and Folk Art* (Minneapolis: Fortress Press, 1997), 31–55.

22. For more on how to "exegete" and deepen understandings of congregation culture(s), see ibid., 56–90.

23. Christine Marie Smith, ed., *Preaching Justice: Ethnic and Cultural Perspectives* (Cleveland: United Church Press, 1998).

24. The team included Bob Songbok Jon, Whitney Rice, Suzanne Wille, and Kimberly Woodbury, all students in the Spring 2008 "Prophetic Preaching" course at Yale Divinity School, taught by Leonora Tubbs Tisdale. Suzanne Wille, then a candidate for ordination in the Episcopal Church, took the lead in compiling this particular list.

25. Brian K. Blount, *Go Preach! Mark's Kingdom Message and the Black Church Today* (Maryknoll, NY: Orbis Books, 1998), 91.

26. Ibid., 178–96.

27. Charles L. Campbell, *The Word before the Powers: An Ethic of Preaching* (Louisville, KY: Westminster John Knox Press, 2002), 77.

28. Ibid., 81.

29. Ibid.

30. Don E. Saliers, *Worship as Theology: Foretaste of Divine Glory* (Nashville: Abingdon Press, 1994), 50. Italics added for emphasis.

31. Thomas G. Long, *Preaching from Memory to Hope* (Louisville, KY: Westminster John Knox Press, 2009), 125.

32. Ibid.,129.

33. Mary Catherine Hilkert, *Naming Grace: Preaching and the Sacramental Imagination* (New York: Continuum, 1998), 83–84.

34. Brad R. Braxton, "Three Questions about Prophets: Who, Why, and How?" in *The African American Pulpit* 11, no. 4 (Fall 2008): 10.

35. Lischer, *Preacher King*, 184–90.

Bibliography

Books, Articles, and Media

Alling, Roger, and David J. Schlafer, eds. *Preaching as Prophetic Calling: Sermons That Work XII.* Harrisburg, PA: Morehouse Publishing, 2004.

Bader-Saye, Scott. *Following Jesus in a Culture of Fear.* Grand Rapids: Brazos Press, 2007.

Blount, Brian K. *Go Preach! Mark's Kingdom Message and the Black Church Today.* Maryknoll, NY: Orbis Books, 1998.

———— and Gary W. Charles. *Preaching Mark in Two Voices.* Louisville, KY: Westminster John Knox Press, 2002.

Boesak, Allan. *Walking on Thorns: The Call to Christian Obedience.* Geneva: World Council of Churches, 1984.

Braxton, Brad. "Three Questions about Prophets: Who, Why, and How?" *The African American Pulpit* 11, no. 4 (Fall 2008): 8–10.

Brueggemann, Walter. *The Prophetic Imagination.* Philadelphia: Fortress Press, 1978.

Burghardt, Walter J., SJ. *Speak the Word with Boldness: Homilies for Risen Christians.* New York: Paulist Press, 1994.

Campbell, Charles L. *The Word before the Powers: An Ethic of Preaching.* Louisville, KY: Westminster John Knox Press, 2002.

Childs, James M., Jr. *Preaching Justice: The Ethical Vocation of Word and Sacrament Ministry.* Harrisburg, PA.: Trinity Press International, 2000.

Clader, Linda L. *Voicing the Vision: Imagination and Prophetic Preaching.* Harrisburg, PA: Morehouse Publishing, 2003.

Coffin, William Sloane. *The Collected Sermons of William Sloane Coffin: The Riverside Years,* Vol. 1. Louisville, KY: Westminster John Knox Press, 2008.

————. *The Collected Sermons of William Sloane Coffin: The Riverside Years,* Vol. 2. Louisville, KY: Westminster John Knox Press, 2008.

————. *Credo.* Louisville, KY: Westminster John Knox Press, 2004.

————. *The Heart Is a Little to the Left: Essays on Public Morality.* Hanover, NH: University Press of New England, 1999.

González, Justo L., and Catherine G. González. *Liberation Preaching: The Pulpit and the Oppressed.* Edited by William D. Thompson. Nashville: Abingdon Press, 1980.

Heschel, Abraham J. *The Prophets*. 2 vols. New York: Harper & Row, 1962.

Hess, Carol Lakey. *Caretakers of Our Common House: Women's Development in Communities of Faith*. Nashville: Abingdon Press, 1997.

Hessel, Dieter T. *Social Ministry*. Rev. ed. Louisville, KY: Westminster/John Knox Press, 1992.

Hilkert, Mary Catherine. *Naming Grace: Preaching and the Sacramental Imagination*. New York: Continuum, 1998.

Hinnant, Olive Elaine. *God Comes Out: A Queer Homiletic*. Cleveland: Pilgrim Press, 2007.

Jeter, Joseph R., Jr. *Crisis Preaching: Personal & Public*. Nashville: Abingdon Press, 1998.

Keillor, Garrison. *Lake Wobegon U.S.A.: Fertility*. Audio CD. Highbridge Audio, 1993.

Kim, Eunjoo Mary. *Women Preaching: Theology and Practice Through the Ages*. Cleveland: Pilgrim Press, 2004.

King, Martin Luther, Jr. *A Knock at Midnight: Inspiration from the Great Sermons of Reverend Martin Luther King, Jr.* Edited by Clayborne Carson and Peter Holloran. New York: Time Warner, 1998.

———. *The Papers of Martin Luther King, Jr.* Vol. 6: *Advocate of the Social Gospel, September 1948–March 1968*. Edited by Clayborne Carson. Berkeley: University of California Press, 2007.

———. *Strength to Love*. Philadelphia: Fortress Press, 1981.

LaRue, Cleophus J., ed. *More Power in the Pulpit: How America's Most Effective Black Preachers Prepare Their Sermons*. Louisville, KY: Westminster John Knox Press, 2009.

———. *Power in the Pulpit: How America's Most Effective Black Preachers Prepare Their Sermons*. Louisville, KY: Westminster John Knox Press, 2002.

Lischer, Richard. *The Preacher King: Martin Luther King, Jr., and the Word That Moved America*. New York: Oxford University Press, 1995.

Long, Thomas G. *Preaching from Memory to Hope*. Louisville, KY: Westminster John Knox Press, 2009.

———. *The Witness of Preaching*. 2nd ed. Louisville, KY: Westminster John Knox Press, 2005.

Lundblad, Barbara K. *Marking Time: Preaching Biblical Stories in Present Tense*. Nashville: Abingdon Press, 2007.

———. *Transforming the Stone: Preaching Through Resistance to Change*. Nashville: Abingdon Press, 2001.

McClure, John S. *Preaching Words: 144 Key Terms in Homiletics*. Louisville, KY: Westminster John Knox Press, 2007.

McMickle, Marvin A. "Prophetic Preaching in the 21st Century: It Is Not Just About the Words." *The African American Pulpit* 11, no. 4 (Fall 2008): 16–18.

———. *Where Have All the Prophets Gone? Reclaiming Prophetic Preaching in America*. Cleveland: Pilgrim Press, 2006.

Mitchell, Ella Pearson, and Valerie Bridgeman Davis, ed. *Those Preaching Women: A Multicultural Collection.* Valley Forge, PA.: Judson Press, 2008.

Nichols, J. Randall. *The Restoring Word: Preaching as Pastoral Communication.* San Francisco: Harper & Row, 1987.

Ottoni-Wilhelm, Dawn. "God's Word in the World: Prophetic Preaching and the Gospel of Jesus Christ." In *Anabaptist Preaching: A Conversation Between Pulpit, Pew & Bible.* Edited by David B. Greiser and Michael A. King, 76–93. Telford, PA: Cascadia Publishing House, 2003.

Paris, Peter J., John W. Cook, James Hudnut-Beumler, Lawrence H. Mamiya, Leonora Tubbs Tisdale, and Judith Weisenfeld. *The History of the Riverside Church in the City of New York.* New York: New York University Press, 2004.

Powery, Luke A. "Walkin' the Talk: The Spirit and the Lived Sermon." *The African American Pulpit* 11, no. 4 (Fall 2008): 20–22.

Resner, André, Jr., ed. *Just Preaching: Prophetic Voices for Economic Justice.* St. Louis: Chalice Press, 2003.

Schlafer, David J., and Timothy F. Sedgwick. *Preaching What We Practice: Proclamation and Moral Discernment.* Harrisburg, PA.: Morehouse Publishing, 2007.

Sherry, Paul H., ed. *The Riverside Preachers.* New York: Pilgrim Press, 1978.

Shriver, Donald W., Jr. *Honest Patriots: Loving a Country Enough to Remember Its Misdeeds.* New York: Oxford University Press, 2005.

Smith, Christine M. *Preaching as Weeping, Confession, and Resistance: Radical Responses to Radical Evil.* Louisville, KY: Westminster/John Knox Press 1992.

Smith, Christine Marie, ed. *Preaching Justice: Ethnic and Cultural Perspectives.* Cleveland: United Church Press, 1998.

Smith, Kelly Miller. *Social Crisis Preaching: The Lyman Beecher Lectures 1983.* Macon, GA: Mercer University Press, 1984.

Steimle, Edmund A., Morris J. Niedenthal, and Charles L. Rice, *Preaching the Story.* Philadelphia: Fortress Press, 1980.

Tisdale, Leonora Tubbs. *Preaching as Local Theology and Folk Art.* Minneapolis: Fortress Press, 1997.

Vos, Cas J. A., Lucy L. Hogan, Johan H. Cilliers, eds. *Preaching as a Language of Hope. Studia Homiletica* 6. Pretoria: Protea Book House, 2007.

Ward, James, and Christine Ward. *Preaching from the Prophets.* Nashville: Abingdon Press, 1995.

West, Cornel. *Democracy Matters: Winning the Fight Against Imperialism.* New York: Penguin Press, 2004.

Wogaman, J. Philip. *Speaking the Truth in Love: Prophetic Preaching to a Broken World.* Louisville, KY: Westminster John Knox Press, 1998.

Sermons

Allen, Ronald J. "Come, Sophia." In *The Teaching Sermon,* 105–9. Nashville: Abingdon Press, 1995.

Bartlett, David. "Woe to Us." *Journal for Preachers* 31, no. 2 (Lent 2008): 33–34.

Black Johnston, Scott. "Blessing and Cursing." Unpublished sermon preached at Trinity Presbyterian Church, Atlanta, GA, July 17, 2005.

Blount, Brian K. "God on the Loose." In *Preaching Mark in Two Voices*, by Brian K. Blount and Gary W. Charles, 28–36. Louisville, KY: Westminster John Knox Press, 2002.

———. "Stay Close." In Blount and Charles, *Preaching Mark in Two Voices*, 170–80.

Boesak, Allan. "Prophetic Faithfulness." In *Best Sermons 3*, edited by James Cox, 149–56. San Francisco: Harper Collins, 1990.

Burghardt, Walter, SJ. "God's Justice and America's Sixth Child." In *Just Preaching: Prophetic Voices for Economic Justice*, edited by André Resner Jr., 131–36. St. Louis: Chalice Press, 2003.

Campbell, Ernest T. "The Case for Reparations." In *The Riverside Preachers*, edited by Paul H. Sherry, 118–24. New York: Pilgrim Press, 1978.

———. "An Open Letter to Billy Graham." In Sherry, ed. *The Riverside Preachers*, 125–31.

———. "Overheard in Room 738." In Sherry, ed. *The Riverside Preachers*, 110–17.

Coffin, William Sloane. "And Pray for the Iranians, Too." In *The Collected Sermons of William Sloane Coffin: The Riverside Years*, Vol. 1, 270–72. Louisville, KY: Westminster John Knox Press, 2008.

———. "Report from Tehran." In *The Collected Sermons of William Sloane Coffin: The Riverside Years*, 1: 272–79.

———. "Warring Madness." In Sherry, ed. *The Riverside Preachers*, 154–59.

———, and Jim Johnson. "AIDS." In *The Collected Sermons of William Sloane Coffin: The Riverside Years*, Vol. 2, 353–58. Louisville, KY: Westminster John Knox Press, 2008.

Davis, Holly Haile. "Three Moons in My Moccasins." In *Those Preaching Women: A Multicultural Collection*, edited by Ella Pearson Mitchell and Valerie Bridgeman Davis, 115–20. Valley Forge, PA.: Judson Press, 2008.

Durber, Susan. "The Massacre of the Innocents." In *Silence in Heaven: A Book of Women's Preaching*, edited by Susan Durber and Heather Walton, 110–15. London: SCM Press, 1994.

Forbes, James A., Jr. "Emancipation from Poverty." In *Just Preaching: Prophetic Voices for Social Justice*, edited by Andrè Resner Jr., 111–18. St. Louis: Chalice Press, 2003.

———. Untitled sermon (Chapter 3). Paraphrased from videotape by Barbara K. Lundblad, *Transforming the Stone: Preaching Through Resistance to Change*, 53–54. Nashville: Abingdon Press, 2001.

Fosdick, Harry Emerson. "The Unknown Soldier." In Sherry, ed. *The Riverside Preachers*, 49–58.

Fry Brown, Teresa L. "Justice or Just Us?" Unpublished sermon preached at
    Trinity Presbyterian Church, Atlanta, GA, November 2, 2007, as part of the
    national conference of the Covenant Network of Presbyterians.
Goines, Veronica. "Neckbone Faith." In *More Power in the Pulpit: How America's Most Effective Black Preachers Prepare Their Sermons,* edited by Cleophus
    J. LaRue, 52–57. Louisville, KY: Westminster John Knox Press, 2009.
Hart-Andersen, Timothy. "The Prophetic Voice of the Church." Unpublished
    sermon preached at Westminster Presbyterian Church, Minneapolis, MN,
    January 28, 2007.
King, Martin Luther, Jr., "How Should a Christian View Communism?" In
    Strength to Love, 97–106. Philadelphia: Fortress Press, 1981.
———. "Loving Your Enemies." In *Strength to Love,* 49–57.
———. "Paul's Letter to American Christians." *The Papers of Martin Luther
    King, Jr.* Vol. 6: *Advocate of the Social Gospel, September 1948–March 1963.*
    Edited by Clayborne Carson. Berkeley: University of California Press, 2007.
Lundblad, Barbara K. "An Easy Chair at the Laundromat." In *Transforming the
    Stone,* 113–19.
———. "No Small Thing." In *Transforming the Stone,* 133–38.
Murtha, Susan, and Sharon Cody. "Finding the Right Well." Unpublished sermon preached at First Congregational Church, Guilford, CT, February 24,
    2008.
Nelson-McJilton, Sheila. "Crumbs." In *Preaching as Prophetic Calling: Sermons
    That Work XII,* edited by Roger Alling and David J. Schlafer, 100–103. Harrisburg, PA: Morehouse Publishing, 2004.
Rice, Whitney. "The Blood That Cries Out from the Ground." Unpublished
    sermon preached in Nouwen Chapel, Yale Divinity School, New Haven, CT,
    May 2008.
Sharp, Carolyn J. "Refuse to Be Consoled." Unpublished sermon preached in
    Marquand Chapel, Yale Divinity School, New Haven, CT, September 8,
    2005.
Tisdale, Leonora Tubbs. "Beautiful Feet and Labor Pains." Unpublished sermon
    preached at Union Theological Seminary, Richmond, VA, February 2, 1988.
Townes, Emilie. "The Valley before the Vision." Unpublished sermon preached
    in Marquand Chapel, Yale Divinity School, New Haven, CT, October 7,
    2005.
Ufford-Chase, Rick. "Reflections from the Moderator." Unpublished sermon
    preached at Fifth Avenue Presbyterian Church in New York City, December
    4, 2005.

Index

action structure in prophetic
    preaching, 76–77
activism. *See* justice advocacy;
    prophetic action; spirituality for
    activism
African Americans
    and civil rights movement, xi, 20,
        39, 75, 92
    demise of prophetic preaching
        and, 1–2
    as pastors, xii, 1, 33
    prejudice and discrimination
        against, 75, 99
    reparations for, 38, 96–98, 101
    and Riverside Church (New York
        City), 54
    slavery and, 72–73, 96–98, 101
    See also King, Martin Luther, Jr.;
        race relations
African Methodist Episcopal
    Church, 116n62
"AIDS" (Coffin), 57
"Alex's Death" (Coffin), 59
Allen, Ronald J., 69, 78, 116n57
American Indians. *See* Native
    Americans
Amos, book of, 36, 41, 49, 69–71,
    105
Amos, the prophet, 91, 106
Anabaptist "peace church" tradition,
    4–5

antiwar protests. *See* Vietnam War
Asian Americans, 99

Bader-Saye, Scott, 17, 35, 36
baptism
    infant baptism, 65
    of Jesus Christ, 81–82
Baptist Church, 1–2, 49, 54
Bartlett, David, 49
Beatitudes, 49
Belenky, Mary Field, 110n26
Bethany Christian Seminary
    (Indiana), 4–5
Bible
    marginalization of prophetic
        dimensions of, 11–12, 28
    models for social action in, 76–
        77
    and narrative structure of
        prophetic preaching, 68–69
    prophets in Old Testament, xii,
        7–8, 10, 11, 13, 41, 90, 106
    reconnecting the individual and
        social/corporate worlds in
        interpretation of, 28–29
    See also specific books of the Bible
Black Economic Development
    Conference, 97. *See also* African
    Americans
Black Johnston, Scott, 64–66,
    114n3

"Blessing and Cursing" (Johnston), 64–66
"The Blood That Cries Out from the Ground" (Rice), 66–67
Blount, Brian, 12, 50–51, 81–82, 103–4, 105, 117n64
Blount, Kaylin, 81
Boesak, Allan, 91–92
Boyd, Bernard, xii
Braxton, Brad, 106
Brueggemann, Walter, xiii–xiv, 6–7, 13, 49
Burghardt, Walter, 77, 116n53

Cain and Abel, 66–67
Campbell, Charles, 59–60, 103–4
Campbell, Ernest T., xv, 38, 75–76, 96–97, 101, 116n45
Caretakers of Our Common House (Hess), 16
Carl, William J., 58–59
Carter, Jimmy, 52, 95, 96
"The Case for Reparations" (Campbell), 38, 96–97, 101
Catholic Church. See Roman Catholic Church
Certain Sound of the Trumpet, The (Proctor), 69
charity and good works, 53–55
Childs, James, 19
Chittister, Joan, 21, 22–23
churches. See specific churches and denominations
civil rights movement, xi, 20, 39, 75, 92. See also African Americans; race relations
Cody, Sharon, 55–56
Coffin, William Sloane, Jr.
    "AIDS," 57–58
    "Alex's Death," 59

anti-Vietnam War activism by, 39
career of, before ministry, 39
on Iranian hostage crisis, 95–96
on prayer, 96
as preacher at Riverside Church (New York City), xv, 39, 40, 52–53, 57–59, 95–96
preparation by, for prophetic preaching, 18, 58–59
prophetic witness by generally, 39, 40
on sermon as invitation to dialogue, 64–65
on "Warring Madness," 52–53
Colleges That Change Lives, 25
"Columbus" (Lowell), 4
"Come, Sophia" (Allen), 78
Communism, 69–71
community, 35–36
confession, prayers of, 34
confessional: "Here I Stand," 86–87
Confession of Belhar, 92
conflict
    fear of, 13–15
    positive effects of, 15–16
Congregational Church, 55–56
Corinthians, First Letter to, 28, 75
courage, 17–18, 35, 106
criticism and prophetic witness, xiii, xiv, 10, 13
"Crumbs" (Nelson-McJilton), 71–72

David, King, 68, 91
Davis, Holly Haile, 46, 112–13n9
death, 59, 84–86
debate guidelines, 58
deed and word. See integrity of prophetic witness; prophetic action

Deuteronomy, book of, 77
dialogue, invitation to, 63–66
discernment, prayers of, 33
"Discrimination, the Shame
    of Sunday Morning"
    (McCracken), 38
Duff, Nancy, 58
Duke Divinity School, 59–60
Durber, Susan, 84–86

"An Easy Chair at the Laundromat"
    (Lundblad), 46–47
Ecclesiastes, book of, 15, 23
El Salvador, 59, 92
"Emancipation from Poverty"
    (Forbes), 54–55
Episcopal Church, 66–67
eschatology, 7, 104–5
Esther, Queen, 90
evil, 5, 9, 10, 103
Ezekiel, book of, 48

family systems theory, 49
fear
    Bader-Saye on, 35, 36
    of conflict, 13–15
    courage in face of, 17–18, 35
    of dividing a congregation, 15–16
    pastor's fear of being disliked,
        rejected, or made to pay a price
        for prophetic witness, 16–18,
        50–51
    and prayers of honest confession,
        34
Fifth Avenue Presbyterian Church
    (New York City), xiv, 27–28,
    32–33, 109n6
"Finding the Right Well" (Murtha
    and Cody), 55–56
First Samuel, book of, 68–69

Following Jesus in a Culture of Fear
    (Bader-Saye), 35
Forbes, James A., Jr., xv, xvi, 22, 39–
    40, 45–46, 54–55, 109n5, 111n3
Forman, James, 38, 97
forms of prophetic preaching
    action structure, 76–77
    conclusion on, 87–88
    confessional: "Here I Stand,"
        86–87
    invitation to dialogue, 63–66
    invitation to lament, 82–86
    letter form, 73–76
    narrative structure, 68–69
    play on words, 78–80
    problem–resolution–new
        possibility, 66–67
    Socratic teaching sermon (moving
        from questions to answers),
        77–78
    structure around an image, 71–73
    thesis–antithesis–synthesis, 69–71
    upsetting the equilibrium (moving
        from ease to dis-ease), 80–82
    See also prophetic preaching
Fosdick, Harry Emerson, xv, 24,
    30–31, 37–39, 52–53, 86–87
Francis of Assisi, St., 94
friendship, 68–69
Fry Brown, Teresa, 79–80, 116n62
fundamentalist-modernist
    theological debates, 30
future of God, 8, 13, 104–6

Galatians, Letter to, 79
gay, lesbian, bisexual, and
    transgendered (GLBT) persons,
    38, 45–49, 58, 64–66
gay marriage, 64–66
Genesis, book of, 66–67

genuine versus wrong stumbling blocks, 41–42
Guilford College, 24–25
Giuliani, Rudy, 27
GLBT persons. *See* gay, lesbian, bisexual, and transgendered (GLBT) persons
God
  faithfulness of, 105–6
  future of, 8, 13, 104–6
  justice and, 77, 80
  love of, 5, 39
  passion as gift of, 68
  peace in human souls and, 23
  promises of, 5
  prophets as speaking for, 4, 11, 13, 22, 91
  reactions by, to human fear and pain, 7, 10, 13, 67, 85–86
  Sophia and, 78
  surprise and, 93–94
  See also Jesus Christ; prayer
"God on the Loose" (Blount), 81–82
"God's Justice and America's Sixth Child" (Burghardt), 77
Goines, Veronica, 71, 72–73, 115n29
González, Catherine and Justo, 6
Graham, Billy, 38, 75–76
grief. *See* lament
Gutierrez, Gustavo, 26

Habitat for Humanity, 25–27
Hart-Andersen, Timothy, 51–52
Heifer International, 101
Heschel, Abraham Joshua, 8
Hess, Carol Lakey, 16
Hessel, Dieter, 28
Hilkert, Mary Catherine, 105–6
Hispanic Americans, 6, 99
Holy Spirit, 10, 21, 22, 33, 65

homeless people, 27, 55
Homiletical Plot, The (Lowry), 80–81
homosexuality, 38, 45–46, 47–49, 58, 64–66
hope, xiii–xiv, 10, 105–6
"How Should a Christian View Communism?" (King), 69–71
humility, 10, 18
Hurricane Katrina, 83–84

image, structure around, 71–73
immigrants, 26, 52, 53, 99, 100
infant baptism, 65
integrity of prophetic witness
  preaching the future of God, 104–5
  prophets as harbingers of hope, 105–6
  sermon as call to prophetic action, 98–102
  sermon as reflection on prophetic action, 95–98
  word and deed in witness of preacher, 90–94
  word and deed in witness of sermon and congregation, 95–104
  worship and preaching as prophetic actions, 102–4
  See also prophetic witness
invitation to dialogue, 63–66
invitation to lament, 82–86
"In What Kind of God Do You Believe?" (McCracken), 38
Iranian hostage crisis, 39, 52, 95–96
Isaiah, book of, 2, 36, 79

James, Epistle of, 64–66
Jeremiah, book of, 72–73, 113n20

Jeremiah, the prophet, 90, 106
Jeroboam, King, 91
Jesus Christ
    baptism of, 81–82
    Beatitudes of, 49
    birth of, and massacre of
        innocents, 84–86
    casting out demons by, 50, 102–3
    on economic injustice, 59–60
    entry of, into Jerusalem, 29
    gospel message of, 90
    healing by, 50, 71, 103
    on love and forgiveness of
        enemies, 41–42
    nonviolent resistance and, 103–4
    preaching by, 102–3
    prophetic ministry of, 5–6, 10,
        12, 102–3, 106
    resurrection of, 105–6
    suffering and death of, 68, 106
    and woman at well, 55–56
    and Zacchaeus, 97
John, Gospel of, 55–56, 113n9
Johnson, Jim, 57
Johnson, Lyndon, 95
John the Baptist, 90
Jonathan and David, 68
Joshua, 77
justice advocacy, 5–6, 25–28, 36,
    46, 76–77, 79–80, 89–90, 99–
    102. See also prophetic action;
    prophetic preaching; prophetic
    witness
"Justice or Just Us?" (Brown),
    79–80

Keillor, Garrison, 1
King, Martin Luther, Jr.
    assassination of, xi
    on Communism, 69–71

on love, 41, 75
on "Paul's Letter to American
    Christians," 74–75
persecution and imprisonment of,
    106
on poverty, 54, 55
prophetic witness of generally, 92
on racism, 66
Kissinger, Henry, 96
Korea. See South Korea

lament
    invitation to, 82–86
    prayers of, 34–35
Latinos. See Hispanic Americans
Lazarus and rich man parable,
    46–47
Left Behind book series, 104
lesbians. See gay, lesbian, bisexual,
    and transgendered (GLBT)
    persons
letter form, 73–76
liberation preaching, 5–6
Liberation Preaching (González and
    González), 6
Lischer, Richard, 94
Long, Thomas G., 63, 104–5,
    114n2
love
    of God, 5, 39
    Jesus Christ on, 41–42
    Martin Luther King on, 41, 75
    speaking truth in love, 4, 42–44
Lowell, James Russell, 4
Lowry, Eugene, 80–81
Luke, Gospel of, 46–47, 49, 54, 77,
    96, 97, 113n20
Lundblad, Barbara, 17, 34, 44,
    46–47, 61, 68–69
Luther, Martin, 86, 93

Lutheran Church, 46–47, 68

MacAfee Brown, Robert, 26
maintenance churches, 36
Mandela, Nelson, 92
marginalized people, 25–27, 46–47, 53–55, 83–86, 99. *See also* immigrants
Mark, Gospel of, 12, 29, 50–51, 77, 81–82, 103
Marney, Carlyle, 54
Maryknoll sisters, 92
Mary's Magnificat, 76
"The Massacre of the Innocents" (Durber), 84–86
Matthew, Gospel of, 15, 41, 59–60, 71–72, 76, 83–86
McClure, John, 8
McCracken, Robert James, xv, 24, 37–38
McMickle, Marvin, 1–2, 7–8, 91–93
McMillan, Neil, xii–xiii
Meaning of Prayer, The (Fosdick), 37
Methodist Church, 4, 43
Micah, book of, 2, 36, 79–80
Micah, the prophet, 106
microfinancing, 102
Moon, Timothy and Steven, xiii
Morse, Christopher L., 114n31
Moses, 91
mourning. *See* lament
Murtha, Susan, 55–56

Naomi and Ruth, 68
narrative structure in prophetic preaching, 68–69
Nathan, 91
National Council of Churches, 97

National Vespers radio program, 24, 30
Native Americans, 46, 66–67, 99, 112–13n9
"Neckbone Faith" (Goines), 72–73
Nelson-McJilton, Sheila, 71–72, 115n25
New Testament. *See* Jesus Christ; *and specific books of New Testament*
Nichols, J. Randall, 29–30
Nixon, Richard, xi–xii, 38, 52, 75–76, 96
nonviolent resistance, 103–4. *See also* civil rights movement
"No Small Thing" (Lundblad), 68–69
nuclear disarmament, 52–53, 59

Old Testament. *See* prophets; *and specific books of Old Testament*
"An Open Letter to Billy Graham" (Campbell), 38, 75–76
ordination
of gay men and lesbians, 45–46
of women, 45, 52
Ottoni-Wilhelm, Dawn, 4–5
"Overheard in Room 738" (Campbell), 38

pacifism, 30, 31, 52–53, 86–87. *See also* peace
Paris, Peter, xv
Park Chung Hee, xiii, 90
Parks, Rosa, 92
pastors
concern for parishioners by, 12–13
confessional ("Here I Stand") sermon by, 86–87

discouragement of, at not making a difference, 19–20

and fear of being disliked, rejected, or made to pay a price for prophetic witness, 16–18, 50–51

and fear of conflict, 13–15

and fear of dividing congregation, 15–16

and feelings of inadequacy in addressing prophetic concerns, 18–19

humility of, 10, 18

in maintenance churches, 36

reconnecting pastoral and prophetic in ministry of, 29–31

self-care for, 14–15

and spiritual follow-up to prophetic witness, 31–32

theological expertise of, 18–19

word and deed in prophetic witness of, 90–94

See also prophetic preaching; prophetic witness; strategies for prophetic preaching

Paul, the apostle, 74–75, 79, 106

"Paul's Letter to American Christians" (King), 74–75

peace, 23, 30, 31, 44–45, 52–53, 86–87. See also pacifism

Pentecostal Church, 39, 111n3

Philippians, Letter to, 57, 67, 83–84

play on words, 78–80

poverty, 25–27, 46–47, 53–55, 90, 101–2

prayer

Coffin on, 96

of discernment, 33

at Fifth Avenue Presbyterian Church (New York City),

32–33, 95–96

Fosdick on, 37

of honest confession, 34

Iranian hostage crisis and, 95–96

of mourning and lament, 34–35

prophetic action and, 94

prophetic witness and, 32–35

preaching. See pastors; prophetic preaching

Preaching Christian Doctrine (Carl), 58–59

Preaching Justice (Smith), 6, 99

Preaching the Story (Steimle), 68

Preaching Words (McClure), 8

Presbyterian Church

Fifth Avenue Presbyterian Church (New York City), xiv, 27–28, 32–33, 109n6

immigrants and, 26

reunited Presbyterian Church (U.S.A.), 91

Theological Task Force on Peace, Unity, and Purity of, 16, 110n28

Westminster Presbyterian Church (Minneapolis), 51–52

priestly preaching, 30

Princeton Theological Seminary, 12, 38, 50, 58, 117n64

prison ministry, 55–56

problem–resolution–new possibility form, 66–67

Proctor, Samuel, 69

prophetic action

acknowledgment of, within congregation, 100

brainstorming on ideas for, 101–2

decision on which action to propose, 99

prophetic action (*continued*)
  multiple options versus one
    option for, 99–100
  prayer and, 94
  by preachers, 90–94
  preparation and coordination of
    sermons calling for, 18, 58–59,
    101
  sermon as call to, 98–102
  sermon as reflection on, 95–98
  worship and preaching as, 102–4
Prophetic Imagination, The
  (Brueggemann), xiii–xiv, 6–7
prophetic ministry, 91–94
prophetic preaching
  action structure in, 76–77
  articulating opposing viewpoint
    in fair and accurate manner for,
    58–59
  as call to prophetic action, 98–
    102
  comic and burlesque style for,
    59–60
  confessional ("Here I Stand")
    form of, 86–87
  congregation's history as bridge to
    prophetic vision for its future
    in, 51–53
  definitions of, 3–10, 29–30
  demise of, 1–3
  forms of, 63–88
  genuine versus wrong stumbling
    blocks for, 41–42
  hallmarks of, 9–10
  integrity of, 89–106
  invitation to dialogue and, 63–
    66
  invitation to lament and, 82–86
  inviting someone personally
    involved to assist with 55–57

letter form of, 73–76
liberation preaching and, 5–6
long view of, 60–61
movement from familiar to
  unfamiliar in, 44–46
narrative structure in, 68–69
play on words in, 78–80
problem–resolution–new
  possibility form of, 66–67
public-issues preaching and, 5–6
reconnecting pastoral preaching
  and, 29–31
as reflection on prophetic action,
  95–98
resistances to, 10–20, 50–51
social-justice preaching and, 5–6
Socratic teaching sermon as form
  of, 77–78
speaking truth in love and, 4,
  42–44
spirituality for activism and,
  20–40
standing in shoes of another in,
  46–49
standing with congregation rather
  than opposite congregation in,
  49–51
strategies for, 41–62
structure around an image in,
  71–73
thesis–antithesis–synthesis form
  of, 69–71
upsetting the equilibrium (moving
  from ease to dis-ease) in,
  80–82
using congregation's current
  mission involvement as bridge
  for, 53–55
worship and preaching as
  prophetic actions, 102–4

See also prophetic witness; resistances to prophetic preaching; spirituality for activism; strategies for prophetic preaching

"The Prophetic Voice of the Church" (Hart-Andersen), 51–52

prophetic witness
criticism and, xiii, xiv, 10, 13
definition of, 9
hope and, xiii–xiv, 10, 105–6
integrity of, 89–106
prayer and, 32–35
reconnecting individuals and communities in, 35–36
and reconnecting pastoral and prophetic in ministry, 29–31
reconnecting unique spiritual gifts with, 36–40
spiritual follow-up to, 31–32
and spirituality for activism, 20–40
word and deed in witness of preacher, 90–94
word and deed in witness of sermon and congregation, 95–104
See also prophetic action; prophetic preaching

prophets
courage of, 17–18, 35, 106
as harbingers of hope, xiii–xiv, 10, 105–6
Holy Spirit and, 10, 21
Jesus Christ as, 5–6, 10, 12, 102–3, 106
Keillor on, 1
Old Testament prophets, xii, 7–8, 10, 11, 13, 41, 90, 106
role of, in upsetting equilibrium, 81
as speaking for God, 4, 11, 13, 22, 91
See also prophetic preaching; prophetic witness; *and specific prophets*

Prophets, The (Heschel), 8
Proverbs, book of, 78
Psalms, book of, 57, 67, 83–84
public-issues preaching, 5–6. *See also* prophetic preaching

Quakers, 24–25

race relations
and civil rights movement, xi, 20, 39, 75, 94
commonalities and differences among racial and ethnic minorities, 99
Native Americans and, 66–67, 99
and reparation for African Americans, 38, 96–98, 101
Riverside Church (New York City) and, 54
slavery and, 72–73, 96–98, 101
in South Africa, 60, 91–92
See also African Americans; Hispanic Americans; King, Martin Luther, Jr.; Native Americans

"Refuse to Be Consoled" (Sharp), 83–84
Re-imagining Conference (2000), 77–78
reparations for African Americans, 38, 96–98, 101
"Report from Tehran" (Coffin), 96

resistances to prophetic preaching
  and discouragement at pastor's
    own prophetic witness not
    making a difference, 19–20
  and fear of being disliked,
    rejected, or made to pay a price
    for prophetic witness, 16–18,
    50–51
  and fear of conflict, 13–15
  and fear of dividing a
    congregation, 15–16
  and feelings of inadequacy in
    addressing prophetic concerns,
    18–19
  and marginalization of prophetic
    dimensions of Scripture, 11–12
  and pastoral concern for
    parishioners, 12–13
  reasons for, 10–20
resurrection of Jesus Christ, 105–6
Rice, Whitney, 66–67
Riverside Church (New York City)
  history of, xv, 109n4
  preachers at, xv, 23–24, 30–31,
    37–40, 52–55, 57–59, 64, 75–
    76, 86–87, 109n5, 111n3
  sermons preached at, 38, 52–55,
    57–59, 75–76, 86–87, 95–97,
    101
  and spirituality for activism
    generally, 22, 109n5, 111n3
Roberts, Joe, xii
Roman Catholic Church, 22–23,
  92, 116n53
Romans, Letter to, 74
Romero, Oscar, 92
Ruth and Naomi, 68

Saliers, Don, 104
Sample, Tex, 44–45

sermons. See prophetic preaching;
  and specific preachers and
  sermons
"Shall the Fundamentalists Win?"
  (Fosdick), 52
Sharp, Carolyn J., 83–84
silence, 22–25
simplicity of lifestyle, 89
slavery, 72–73, 96–98, 101. See
  also reparations for African
  Americans
Smith, Christine, 6, 99
Smith, Kelly Miller, 6
social activism. See justice advocacy;
  prophetic action; prophetic
  preaching; spirituality for
  activism
social-justice preaching, 5–6. See
  also justice advocacy; prophetic
  preaching
Socratic teaching sermon, 77–78
solitude, 22–23
Sophia, 78
South Africa, 60, 91–92
South Korea, xiii, 89–90
Speaking the Truth in Love
  (Wogaman), 4, 43–44
speaking truth in love, 4, 42–44
spirituality for activism
  introduction to, 21–22
  Quakers and, 24–25
  reconnecting individuals and
    communities in prophetic
    witness, 35–36
  reconnecting life of solitude
    (silence) and prophetic speech,
    22–25
  reconnecting our lives with
    suffering people, 25–27
  reconnecting pastoral and

prophetic in ministry, 29–31

reconnecting prayer and prophetic witness, 32–35

reconnecting the individual and social/corporate worlds in biblical interpretation, 28–29

reconnecting unique spiritual gifts with visionary, prophetic witness, 36–40

spiritual follow-up to prophetic witness, 31–32

See also Riverside Church (New York City)

Spock, Benjamin, 39

"Stay Close" (Blount), 50–51

strategies for prophetic preaching
articulating opposing viewpoint in fair and accurate manner, 58–59

comic and burlesque style, 59–60

conclusion on, 62

congregation's current mission involvement as bridge for prophetic witness, 53–55

congregation's history as bridge to prophetic vision for its future, 51–53

inviting someone personally involved in concern to preach on it, 55–57

speaking truth in love, 4, 42–44

standing in shoes of another and viewing world from different perspective, 46–49

standing with congregation rather than opposite congregation, 49–51

starting with familiar and moving toward unfamiliar, 44–46

taking the long view, 60–61

See also prophetic preaching

structure around an image, 71–73

stumbling blocks, 41–42

suffering, 25–27, 46–47, 53–55, 83–86. See also justice advocacy; poverty

Teresa, Mother, 89

Theology of Culture (Tillich), 41–42

There Is a Season (Chittister), 21, 23

thesis–antithesis–synthesis form, 69–71

"Three Moons in My Moccasins" (Davis), 46

Tillich, Paul, 41–42

Tittle, Ernest Freemont, 43–44

Townes, Emilie, 47–49

Transforming the Stone (Lundblad), 17, 34

Truth, Sojourner, 92, 106

Tutu, Desmond, 60, 92

Ufford-Chase, Rick, 26

Union Theological Seminary, 68, 79, 117n64

University of North Carolina, xii

"The Unknown Soldier" (Fosdick), 31, 52–53, 86–87

upsetting the equilibrium, 80–82

"The Valley Before the Vision" (Townes), 47–49

Vanderbilt Divinity School, 8

Vietnam War, xi–xiii, 11, 38, 39, 52, 75–76, 90, 95

"Warring Madness" (Coffin), 52–53

Weiss, Cora, 52

West, Cornel, 8–9, 89, 92–93

Westminster Presbyterian Church (Minneapolis), 51–52

"What Is Meant by the Will of God?" (McCracken), 38

Where Have All the Prophets Gone? (McMickle), 1–2, 7–8, 91

"Where Protestants Differ from Roman Catholics and Why" (McCracken), 38

Wink, Walter, 59–60

Winn, Albert Curry, xii

Wogaman, Philip, 4–5, 6, 43–44

women
Jesus Christ and woman at well, 55–56
ordination of, 45, 52
Re-imagining Conference (2000) and, 77–78
transitional program for women prisoners, 55–56

widow demanding justice in Luke's Gospel, 77

Women's Ways of Knowing (Belenky), 110n26

word and deed. *See* integrity of prophetic witness; prophetic action

Word before the Powers, The (Campbell), 103

World Council of Churches, 97

World War I, 30–31, 86–87

World War II, 30, 31

worship as prophetic action, 102–4

Yale Divinity School, 6, 47–49, 82–83, 100, 101

Yale University, 39, 64

Zacchaeus, 38, 97

CPSIA information can be obtained at www.ICGtesting.com
Printed in the USA
LVOW06s1506080913

351501LV00002B/378/P

3 4711 00217 3575

9 780664 233327